The Spelling Toolbox

Workbook 1

Linda Kita-Bradley

Grass Roots Press

Edmonton, Alberta, Canada

2002

The Spelling Toolbox – Workbook 1 is published by

Grass Roots Press
A division of Literacy Services of Canada Ltd.

PHONE	1-780-413-6491
FAX	1-780-413-6582
E-MAIL	info@grassrootsbooks.net
WEB	www.grassrootsbooks.net

AUTHOR	Linda Kita-Bradley
CO-ORDINATOR	Pat Campbell
EDITOR	Judith Tomlinson
COVER DESIGN	Lara Minja – Lime Design
DESIGN	Patsy Price – Far Beyond Words
LAYOUT	Patsy Price, Renate Oddy & Evelyn David – Far Beyond Words
PRINTING	Quality Color Press Inc.

ACKNOWLEDGMENT

The Word Origins were adapted from the following publication:

Hendrickson, R. (1997). *Words and phrase origins.* New York, NY: Checkmark Books.

National Library of Canada Cataloguing in Publication Data

Kita-Bradley, Linda, 1958-
      The spelling toolbox : workbook one

ISBN 978-1-894593-14-4

      1. English language—Orthography and spelling. I. Title

PE1145.2.K57 2002   428.1   C2001-903375-3

Printed in Canada

Contents

About this book

This spelling workbook aims to help adult beginner spellers develop a strategy-based approach to spelling. Although accurate spelling is the final goal, it is important that strategy building remain the focus as you and the learners work through the units in this book.

The first unit in the book introduces the five strategies, or spelling tools that the learners will use throughout the remaining twenty units. The five spelling tools are these:

- *Say, listen, and write.*
- *Make a word family.*
- *Divide and conquer.*
- *Use a spelling rule.*
- *Look for tricky parts.*

Units 2 to 21 begin with a theme-based word list followed by four parts:

■ Working with spelling tools

Learners do a series of spelling exercises that help them recognize how and when the five spelling tools can be used.

■ Trying out your spelling tools

Learners complete two dictations. The first dictation gives the learners a chance to spell the unit words as they appear in the unit word list. The second dictation manipulates the unit words in some way in order to give the learners an opportunity to choose any of the five spelling tools that can help them spell the new word. For example, if "rub" is in the unit word list, then "rubbing" or "scrub" may appear in the second dictation. Common sight words are also introduced in the second dictation.

■ Applying your spelling tools

After looking at an example, learners are asked to do a short piece of writing that relates to the unit theme. They are able to look at their spelling analytically and apply appropriate spelling tools while completing a real writing task.

■ A final word

Learners add spelling words to their personal spelling dictionary.

The workbook also includes the following:

■ Student glossary

The student glossary explains terms that the learner needs to know to complete the spelling exercises.

■ Word list

This list includes all the words that appear in the unit word lists. The list is presented alphabetically and indicates in which unit each word is found.

■ Notes for users

The notes primarily include complete dictations, word families, and explanations of the spelling rules introduced in the workbook.

■ Feature: Word Origins

The origins of various words and sayings are presented throughout the workbook. Whether or not all these stories are completely true, it is hoped that you and the learners will find them both interesting and entertaining.

unit
1

introduction

Spelling Tools

You are going to learn to use five spelling tools.
A spelling tool helps you spell words.

If you use the spelling tools in this book,
you will have a good chance
of spelling new words right . . .

and you will remember how to spell the words, too.

tool 1
Say, listen, and write.

There are many words that you can spell right if you
say the words slowly and
listen to each sound in the word.

Look at the words in the box.

at	no	it
fun	lots	bet
plan	drug	flag

Say each word slowly.
Listen.
You can hear each sound.

Try it out

Say each word.
Listen to each sound.
Write the word as you say it.

pot	*PaT*	pots	*PaTS*
sat	*SaT*	set	*SeT*
lamp	*lamP*	raft	*RaFT*
slap	*SlaP*	slop	*SlOP*

If this spelling tool does not work,
try the next spelling tool.

tool 2
Make a word family.

Words that rhyme
and have the same spelling pattern
belong to the same word family.

For example, the words **make**, **shake**, and **rake** rhyme.
They have the same spelling pattern: **ake**.
So, the words **make**, **shake**, and **rake**
belong to the word family **ake**.

Do you know a word
that rhymes with the word
you are trying to spell?

Try spelling your word the same way.

Say these pairs of words.

| my
by | best
rest | think
drink | funny
sunny | ran
plan | take
bake |

Each pair of words rhymes.
Each word in the pair
is spelled the same way.

Each pair of words is a small word family.

Try it out

Say this word: **row**

Think of words that rhyme.
Write the words.

Your teacher will help you with the spelling.

**Note
1**

_____   row   _____   _____   _____

_____   _____   _____   _____

_____   _____   _____   _____

_____   _____   _____   _____

Look at your words.
Circle the words that belong to the same word family as **row**.

Learn to spell one of these words, and
you will be able to spell
all of the words.

tool 3
Divide and conquer.

If you have to spell a big word,
divide the word into parts.

Look for ❐ common beginning parts
          ❐ common end parts
          ❐ little words in the big word

Some common beginning parts	Some common end parts
re do – redo	**es** box – boxes
un cover – uncover	**ing** leak – leaking
dis like – dislike	**ed** want – wanted
	er farm – farmer
	y stick – sticky
	's my dad – my dad's farm

Try it out

1— Look at the word **remake** in the box.

The beginning part is **re**.
What little word is left?

Find the beginning part
in the other words.

Divide each word.

remake	_re make_
discover	_____
unlike	_____
dismiss	_____
relive	_____
unsafe	_____

2 — Look at the word **mixes** in the box.

The end part is **es**.
What little word is left?

Find the end part
in the other words.
Divide each word.

mixes	mix es
needed	
jumping	
tricky	
runs	
renter	

3 — Look at the word **suntan** in the box.

What little words can you see?
Look at the other words.
Find the little words in each word.
Write the little words on the line.

suntan	sun tan
blowout	
afternoon	
baseball	
bedroom	
rainfall	

4 — Look at the word **carry** in the box.
What little word can you see?

Look at the other words.
Divide each word
by finding the little words.

carry	car ry
become	
yesterday	
Monday	
listen	

Dividing words into parts is a
good spelling tool to use.

But, if this spelling tool does not work,
try the next spelling tool.

tool 4
Use a spelling rule.

In this book, you are going to learn four spelling rules.

The four rules are
1. The *Doubling* rule
2. The *Y* rule
3. The *Silent E* rule
4. The *Drop the E* rule

Here are some examples of each rule.

Note 2

---

1. The *Doubling* rule

rob ⟶ robber / robbed   rub ⟶ rubber / rubbing
stop ⟶ stopped / stopping   fun ⟶ funny

---

2. The *Y* rule

hurry ⟶ hurried / hurrying   cherry ⟶ cherries
play ⟶ plays / playing   family ⟶ families
copy ⟶ copied / copying

---

3. The *Silent E* rule

mad / made   bit / bite   rob / robe
cop / cope   hat / hate   cub / cube

---

4. The *Drop the E* rule

rake ⟶ raked / raking   close ⟶ closer / closed / closing
bike ⟶ biker / biked / biking   hope ⟶ hoped / hoping

You will learn more about these rules.

When you learn these rules,
    you can use them
        to help you spell many new words.

tool 5
Look for tricky parts.

Some words have tricky parts.

Say the words in the box.
Each word has a tricky part.
The tricky part is marked.

th<u>ey</u>	You need two letters to make the long **a** sound.
w<u>h</u>en	The letter **h** is silent.
f<u>ee</u>t	There are two **e**s in this word.
w<u>a</u>sh	The vowel **a** sounds like the short vowel **o**.

How can you learn the tricky parts in a word?

Try these six steps:

1. **Read the word slowly.**

2. **Mark any tricky part.**

3. **Study the tricky part.**

4. **Cover the word.**

5. **Write the word.**

6. **Check your spelling.**

Try it out

1— Look at these words.

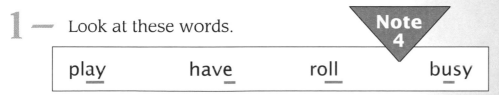

The tricky parts are marked.
Why are these parts tricky?

2 —
Look at the words below.
Look for the tricky parts.
Use the six steps to help you spell each word.

play	_____
have	_____
roll	_____
busy	_____
they	_____
when	_____
feet	_____
wash	_____

Remember to . . .
1. **Read the word slowly.**
2. **Mark any tricky part.**
3. **Study the tricky part.**
4. **Cover the word.**
5. **Write the word.**
6. **Check the spelling.**

**Now you are ready
    to use your new spelling tools.**

Don't count your chickens before they hatch.

Aesop was a great Greek thinker.
He told this story about a woman.

> A woman brought her eggs to the market.
> She wanted to sell her eggs.
> She wanted to make a lot of money.
> The woman planned to buy a goose with the money.
> Then she planned to sell the goose and buy a cow.
> But the woman kicked over her basket.
> The eggs broke. She didn't make a penny.

Aesop's story shows that it's not good
to plan too far ahead.
We get the saying
"*Don't count your chickens before they hatch*"
from this story.

• **word origins** •

Practice words

Sunday	TV	DVD	cards	chat
walk	friends	visit	tea	talk
weekend	rest	park	sun	popcorn

Working with spelling tools

Say, listen, and write.

Say each word.
Listen to each sound.
Write the word as you say it.

TV _____	chat _____	DVD _____
sun _____	rest _____	pop _____

If you say these words slowly,
you will have a good chance
of spelling them right.

Make a word family.

Say these words: **talk   walk**

Think of words that rhyme.
Write the words.
Your teacher will help you with the spelling.

Note 5

talk		
walk		

Look at your words.
Circle the words that belong
to the same word family as **talk** and **walk**.

Learn to spell one of these words, and
you will be able to spell
all of the words.

Divide and conquer.

How can you divide and conquer
these words?

cards	_____
Sunday	_____
visit	_____
weekend	_____
popcorn	_____
friends	_____

Divide and conquer

Do you see
- ☐ **common beginning parts?**
- ☐ **common end parts?**
- ☐ **little words?**

Use a spelling rule.

Look at these words.

sun ⟶	sunny / sunning
chat ⟶	chatty / chatted / chatting
pop ⟶	poppy / popped / popping / popper

What happens
when you add an end part
to **sun, chat** and **pop**?

Practice the *Doubling* rule.

Say the base word.
Add the end part to the base word.
Say the new word.

sun + ing	_sunning_
sun + y	_____
chat + ed	_____
chat + ing	_____
chat + y	_____
pop + ed	_____
pop + ing	_____
pop + y	_____

Doubling rule

**If a word has ONE syllable
and ends with ONE vowel
and ONE consonant,
double the final consonant
when you add an end part
that starts with a vowel.**

Look for tricky parts.

Look at the words below.
Look for the tricky parts.
Use the six steps to help you
spell the words.

friend   _____

park   _____

tea   _____

weekend   _____

Remember to . . .

1. **Read the word slowly.**
2. **Mark any tricky part.**
3. **Study the tricky part.**
4. **Cover the word.**
5. **Write the word.**
6. **Check the spelling.**

Trying out your spelling tools

1— Your teacher will read a paragraph.
Listen.
Finish the ideas.

Note 6

① I _____ every _____.

② I like to _____ my _____.

③ We _____ over _____ or
play _____. ④ We don't like
_____, but we like _____.

⑤ We make a big bowl of _____ and
_____. ⑥ Sometimes, we go to
the _____ and hang out in the
_____. ⑦ I love the _____.
It's my time to _____.

Use your spelling tools.

Say, listen, and write.

Make a word family.

Divide and conquer.

Use a spelling rule.

Look for tricky parts.

2— Check your spelling.
Your teacher will help you.

Which words gave you trouble?
Use a different spelling tool.
Try again.

3— Your teacher will read another paragraph.
You are going to spell new words.
This will give you a chance
to try out your spelling tools.

Note
7

① The _____ day of _____
week is _____. ② My _____
_____ me _____ she can.
③ It's _____ by the time she goes
home. ④ She's always _____ for the
_____. ⑤ She's so _____.
⑥ My life would seem _____
without her.

**Use your
spelling tools.**

Say, listen, and write.

Make a word family.

Divide and conquer.

Use a spelling rule.

Look for tricky parts.

4— Check your spelling.
Your teacher will help you.

Which words gave you trouble?
Use a different spelling tool.
Try again.

Applying your spelling tools

1— Look at this example.

Lil went to see Clark.
Clark was not home.

Here is the note
that Lil left for Clark.

Hi

Sorry I missed you.
Come over later to
watch a DVD.

Lil

2— Your turn.

Your friend's phone is out of order.

Invite your friend to do something.

A final word

Which words about *leisure* would you like to add to your dictionary?

bite the bullet

In the 1850s, rifles had paper tubes.
The paper tubes were filled with gunpowder.
Soldiers had to bite open the tube
to make the gun work.
The soldiers had to stay calm
when they bit open the tube.
Today, *bite the bullet* means
to stay calm when there is a problem.

Practice words

fun	wish	see	baby	girl
note	love	birthday	come	made
party	together	here	happy	time

Working with spelling tools

 ## Say, listen, and write.

Say each word.
Listen to each sound.
Write the word as you say it.

wish _____	fun _____

If you say these words slowly,
you will have a good chance
of spelling them right.

Make a word family.

Say this word: **see**

Think of words that rhyme.
Write the words.
Your teacher will help you with the spelling.

Note 8

see _____ _____

_____ _____ _____

_____ _____ _____

_____ _____ _____

_____ _____ _____

Look at your words.
Circle the words that belong
to the same word family as **see**.

Learn to spell one of these words, and
you will be able to spell
all of the words.

Divide and conquer.

How can you divide and conquer
these words?

together _____

birthday _____

Divide and conquer

Do you see
❑ **common beginning parts?**
❑ **common end parts?**
❑ **little words?**

Use a spelling rule.

Say these words: **baby   party   happy**

How many syllables do you hear?

Listen to the end sound.
What sound do you hear?

Practice the Y rule (part 1).

Say the word.
Divide the word into two syllables.
Underline the letter that makes
the long **e** sound.

baby	ba b<u>y</u>
party	
happy	

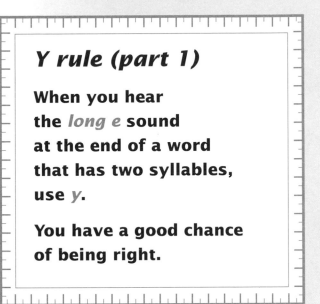

Y rule (part 1)

**When you hear
the *long e* sound
at the end of a word
that has two syllables,
use *y*.**

**You have a good chance
of being right.**

Look at these words.

baby	➤ babying / babied
party	➤ partying / partied / partier
happy	➤ happier

What happens when you
add **ing** to baby and party?

What happens when you
add **ed** or **er** to all the base words?

Y rule (part 2)

**If a word ends in
consonant + y,
the *y* changes to *i*
when you add all end parts
except *ing*.**

Practice the _Y_ rule (part 2).

Say the base word.
Add the end part to the base word.
Say the new word.

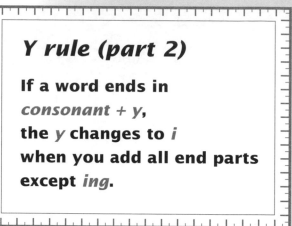

Y rule (part 2)

If a word ends in
consonant + y,
the _y_ changes to _i_
when you add all end parts
except _ing_.

happ**y** + er	_happier_
party + ed	
party + er	
party + ing	
party + s*	
baby + ed	
baby + ing	
baby + s*	

* Change the **y** to **i** and add **es**.
You always need to add **es**—not only **s**—
so that the word sounds right.
Compare **partis** and **parties**,
babis and **babies**.

Your teacher will read
these pairs of words.
Listen.

Tim	not	mad	her
time	note	made	here

What happens
to the short vowel sound
in a word
when you add **e**
to the end of the word?

Silent E rule

When you add the letter _e_
to the end of a word,
the short vowel sound in that word
changes to a long vowel sound.

Practice the *Silent E* rule.

Say the base word.
Add the letter **e.**
Say the new word.

Tim + e	*time*
not + e	_____
mad + e	_____
her + e	_____

> ### Silent E rule
>
> **When you add the letter *e*
> to the end of a word,
> the short vowel sound
> in that word changes to
> a long vowel sound.**

Look at the words below.
What happens when you add **ed**, **ing** or **er**?

love	⟶ loved / loving / lover
time	⟶ timed / timing / timer
note	⟶ noted / noting
come	⟶ coming

Practice the *Drop the E* rule.

Say the base word.
Cross out the silent **e**.
Add the end part to the base word.

> ### Drop the E rule
>
> **If your word ends with
> a *silent e*,
> drop the *silent e*
> before you add an end part
> that starts with a vowel.**

tim~~e~~	+ ed	*timed*
time	+ er	_____
time	+ ing	_____
love	+ ed	_____
love	+ ing	_____
love	+ er	_____
come	+ ing	_____
note	+ ed	_____
note	+ ing	_____

Look for tricky parts.

Look at the words below.
Look for the tricky parts.
Use the six steps to help you
spell the words.

love _____

girl _____

birthday _____

come _____

Remember to . . .

1. **Read the word slowly.**
2. **Mark any tricky part.**
3. **Study the tricky part.**
4. **Cover the word.**
5. **Write the word.**
6. **Check the spelling.**

Trying out your spelling tools

1— Your teacher will read some sentences.
Listen.
Finish the sentences.

Note 9

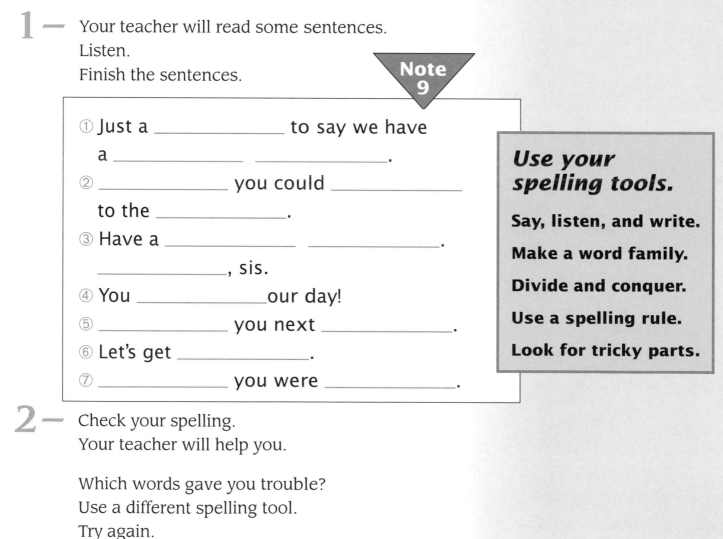

① Just a _____ to say we have

a _____ _____.

② _____ you could _____

to the _____.

③ Have a _____ _____.

_____, sis.

④ You _____our day!

⑤ _____ you next _____.

⑥ Let's get _____.

⑦ _____ you were _____.

**Use your
spelling tools.**

Say, listen, and write.

Make a word family.

Divide and conquer.

Use a spelling rule.

Look for tricky parts.

2— Check your spelling.
Your teacher will help you.

Which words gave you trouble?
Use a different spelling tool.
Try again.

3— Your teacher will read
some more sentences.

You are going to spell new words.
This will give you a chance
to try out your spelling tools.

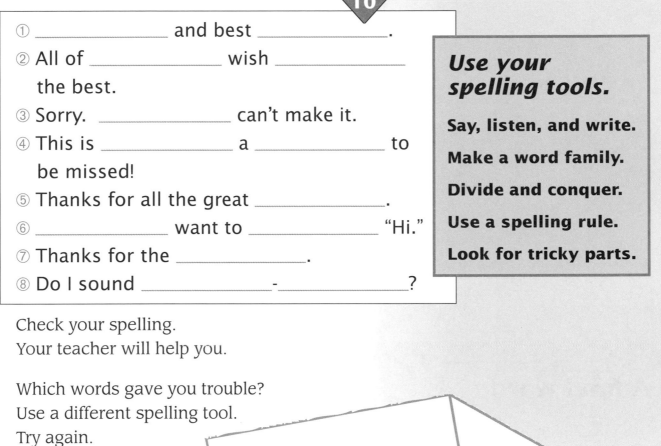

① _____ and best _____.

② All of _____ wish _____
the best.

③ Sorry. _____ can't make it.

④ This is _____ a _____ to
be missed!

⑤ Thanks for all the great _____.

⑥ _____ want to _____ "Hi."

⑦ Thanks for the _____.

⑧ Do I sound _____-_____?

Note 10

Use your spelling tools.

Say, listen, and write.

Make a word family.

Divide and conquer.

Use a spelling rule.

Look for tricky parts.

Check your spelling.
Your teacher will help you.

Which words gave you trouble?
Use a different spelling tool.
Try again.

Applying your spelling tools

1— Look at this example.

It's Lee's birthday.

Granny sends her
a birthday wish.

Happy Birthday!

Have a great day, Lee.
I wish I could be there.

Love,
Granny

2— Your turn.

Send a birthday card.

Add a personal
birthday wish.

A final word

Which words about **family times**
would you like to add
to your dictionary?

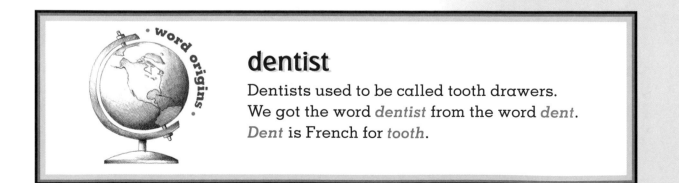

dentist
Dentists used to be called tooth drawers.
We got the word *dentist* from the word *dent*.
Dent is French for *tooth*.

Practice words

some	coffee	jam	bread	eggs
box	hotdogs	package	bunch	fruit
bag	milk	shampoo	carton	few

Working with spelling tools

Say, listen, and write.

Say each word.
Listen to each sound.
Write the word as you say it.

bag _____	jam _____	bunch _____
box _____	milk _____	

If you say these words slowly,
you will have a good chance
of spelling them right.

Make a word family.

Say this word: **bread**

Think of words that rhyme.
Write the words.
Your teacher will help you with the spelling.

Note 11

bread _____ _____

_____ _____ _____

_____ _____ _____

Look at your words.
Circle the words that belong
to the same word family as **bread**.

Learn to spell one of these words, and
you will be able to spell
all of the words.

Divide and conquer.

How can you divide and conquer
these words?

coffee _____
hotdogs _____
package _____
shampoo _____
carton _____
eggs _____

Divide and conquer

Do you see
- ☐ common beginning parts?
- ☐ common end parts?
- ☐ little words?

Use a spelling rule.

Practice the **Doubling** rule.

Say the base word.
Add the end part to the base word.
Say the new word.

bag + ed   _____

bag + ing   _____

bag + y   _____

bag + er   _____

bag + s   _____

jam + ed   _____

jam + ing   _____

jam + s   _____

Doubling rule

If a word has ONE syllable and ends with ONE vowel and ONE consonant, double the final consonant when you add an end part that starts with a vowel.

Look for tricky parts.

Look at the words below.
Look for the tricky parts.
Use the six steps to help you
spell the words.

some   _____

egg   _____

fruit   _____

few   _____

package   _____

Remember to...

1. Read the word slowly.

2. Mark any tricky part.

3. Study the tricky part.

4. Cover the word.

5. Write the word.

6. Check the spelling.

Trying out your spelling tools

1— Your teacher will read a shopping list.
Listen. Finish the list.

Note 12

① a package of _____ and a _____ of chips

② a dozen _____ and a _____ of _____

③ _____ _____ and lots of _____

④ a loaf of _____ and a _____ bars of soap

⑤ jar of _____, _____ of soup,
   one _____ of cereal

⑥ a bottle of _____

2— Check your spelling.
Your teacher will help you.

Which words gave you trouble?
Use a different spelling tool. Try again.

3— Your teacher will read another shopping list.
You are going to spell new words.
This will give you a chance
to try out your spelling tools.

Note 13

Use your spelling tools.

Say, listen, and write.

Make a word family.

Divide and conquer.

Use a spelling rule.

Look for tricky parts.

① something that goes _____

② a _____ of _____ chips

③ a bunch of _____

④ five _____ _____ green onions

⑤ a _____ of _____ mix

⑥ _____ ham

4— Check your spelling.
Your teacher will help you.

Which words gave you trouble?
Use a different spelling tool.
Try again.

Applying your spelling tools

1— Look at this example.

Linda is planning
a surprise barbecue
for her husband.

This is her shopping list.

How many people
do you think
Linda is expecting?

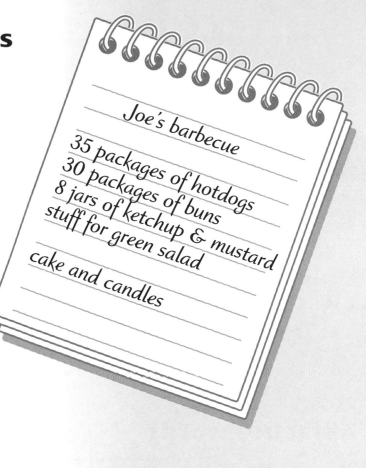

Joe's barbecue

35 packages of hotdogs
30 packages of buns
8 jars of ketchup & mustard
stuff for green salad

cake and candles

2— Your turn.

Plan a party.
Write your shopping list.

A final word

Which words about **shopping**
would you like to add
to your dictionary?

unit 5

home

Fix It Up

Practice words

fix	pay	please	rip	remove
leaky	paint	check	plug	clean
clog	draft	replace	can	old

Working with spelling tools

Say, listen, and write.

Say each word.
Listen to each sound.
Write the word as you say it.

fix	_____	rip	_____	clog	_____
draft	_____	old	_____	plug	_____

If you say these words slowly,
you will have a good chance
of spelling them right.

Make a word family.

Say this word: **check**

Think of words that rhyme.
Write the words.
Your teacher will help you with the spelling.

Note 14

check _____ _____
_____ _____ _____
_____ _____ _____

Look at your words.
Circle the words that belong to the same word family as **check**.

Learn to spell one of these words, and
you will be able to spell
all of the words.

Say this word: **place**

Think of words that rhyme.
Write the words.
Your teacher will help you with the spelling.

Note 15

place _____ _____
_____ _____ _____
_____ _____ _____
_____ _____ _____

Look at your words.
Circle the words that belong to the same word family as **place**.

Learn to spell one of these words, and
you will be able to spell
all of the words.

Say this word: **pay**

Think of words that rhyme.
Write the words.
Your teacher will help you with the spelling.

Note 16

pay _____   _____   _____

_____   _____   _____

_____   _____   _____

_____   _____   _____

Look at your words.
Circle the words that belong to the same word family as **pay**.

Learn to spell one of these words, and
you will be able to spell
all of the words.

Divide and conquer.

How can you divide and conquer
these words?

remove _____
leaky _____
replace _____

Divide and conquer.

Do you see
❑ **common beginning parts?**
❑ **common end parts?**
❑ **little words?**

April

The Latin word *aperia* means *open*.
Romans noticed that flowers
opened in the spring.
They called that time of spring *April*.

word origins

Use a spelling rule.

Practice the *Doubling* rule.

Say the base word.
Add the end part to the base word.
Say the new word.

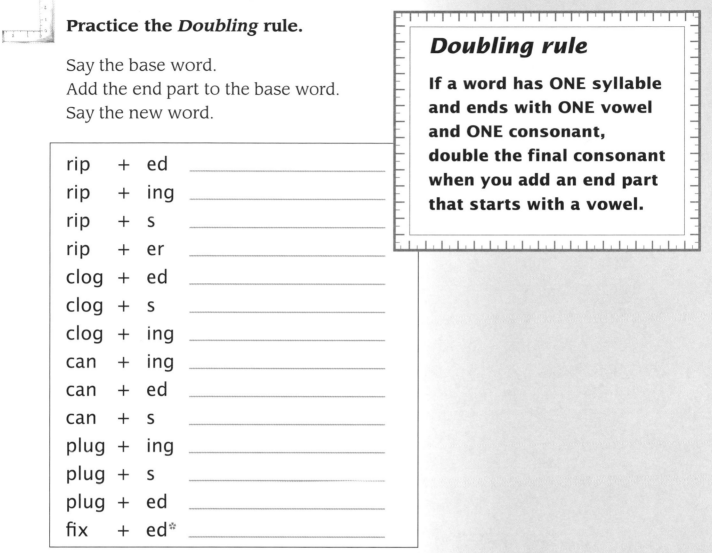

rip	+ ed	_____
rip	+ ing	_____
rip	+ s	_____
rip	+ er	_____
clog	+ ed	_____
clog	+ s	_____
clog	+ ing	_____
can	+ ing	_____
can	+ ed	_____
can	+ s	_____
plug	+ ing	_____
plug	+ s	_____
plug	+ ed	_____
fix	+ ed*	_____

Doubling rule

If a word has ONE syllable and ends with ONE vowel and ONE consonant, double the final consonant when you add an end part that starts with a vowel.

*Do not use the *Doubling* rule with the letter **x**.
You never see **xx** in English spelling.

Practice the *Silent E* rule.

Say the word.
Underline the long vowel sound.
Circle the silent **e**.

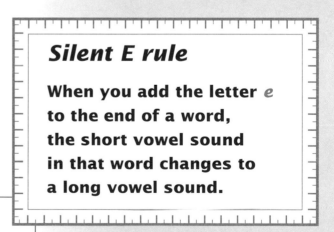

replace

Silent E rule

When you add the letter *e* to the end of a word, the short vowel sound in that word changes to a long vowel sound.

Practice the *Drop the E* rule.

Say the base word.
Add the end part to the base word.
Say the new word.

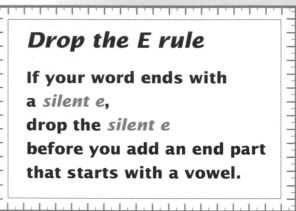

Drop the E rule

If your word ends with
a *silent e*,
drop the *silent e*
before you add an end part
that starts with a vowel.

replace	+ ed	_____
replace	+ ing	_____
replace	+ s	_____
remove	+ ed	_____
remove	+ ing	_____
remove	+ er	_____
remove	+ s	_____
please	+ ed	_____
please	+ ing	_____
please	+ s	_____

Look for tricky parts.

Look at the words below.
Look for the tricky parts.
Use the six steps to help you
spell the words.

paint	_____
clean	_____
please	_____
leak	_____
move	_____

Remember to . . .

1. Read the word slowly.
2. Mark any tricky part.
3. Study the tricky part.
4. Cover the word.
5. Write the word.
6. Check the spelling.

Trying out your spelling rules

1 — Your teacher will read a letter.
Listen. Finish the letter.

▼ Note 17

Use your spelling tools.

Say, listen, and write.

Make a word family.

Divide and conquer.

Use a spelling rule.

Look for tricky parts.

Hi Dad,
I'm finally in my new place,
but I'm not very happy!

① I have to _____ and _____ everything. ② The sink has a _____. I can't _____ it. ③ The _____ is _____ and dirty. ④ The rug is all _____. It has a big _____. ⑤ I have to _____ the windows because there is a big _____. ⑥ The tub is _____. It has no _____. ⑦ I still have to _____ a lot of things.

⑧ How can I _____ for these things? _____ help!

Your sad, sad son,
Jay

2 — Check your spelling. Your teacher will help you.

Which words gave you trouble?
Use a different spelling tool. Try again.

3 — Your teacher will read a fix-it list.
You are going to spell new words.
This will give you a chance
to try out your spelling tools.

Check your spelling.
Your teacher will help you.

Which words gave you trouble?
Use a different spelling tool.
Try again.

▼ Note 18

① fix the _____
② fix _____ sink
③ fix _____ curtain
④ fix _____ drain
⑤ fix _____ door
⑥ fix _____ stairs
⑦ _____ walls
⑧ _____ walls

Applying your spelling tools

1– Look at this example.

Here is a note
that Alan left
for the building manager.

> The sink in my bathroom
> is still leaking. The water is
> dripping all over the place.
> Can you <u>please</u> fix it today?
>
> Alan
> Apt. 4

2– Your turn.

You have a problem
with your apartment.

Leave a note on the
building manager's door.

A final word

Which words about **fix-it-up**
would you like to add
to your dictionary?

Practice words

thank	notice	one	pack	month
carry	boxes	gas	lug	rent
heat	move	look	cry	you

Working with spelling tools

Say, listen, and write.

Say each word.
Listen to each sound.
Write the word as you say it.

rent _____	boxes _____
gas _____	lug _____

If you say these words slowly,
you will have a good chance
of spelling them right.

Make a word family.

Say this word: **pack**

Think of words that rhyme.
Write the words.
Your teacher will help you with the spelling.

Note 19

pack _____ _____
_____ _____ _____
_____ _____ _____
_____ _____ _____

Look at your words.
Circle the words that belong
to the same word family as **pack**.

Learn to spell one of these words, and
you will be able to spell
all of the words.

Say this word: **look**

Think of words that rhyme.
Write the words.
Your teacher will help you with the spelling.

Note 20

look _____ _____
_____ _____ _____
_____ _____ _____

Look at your words.
Circle the words that belong
to the same word family as **look**.

Learn to spell one of these words, and
you will be able to spell
all of the words.

Say this word: **cry**

Think of words that rhyme.
Write the words.
Your teacher will help you with the spelling.

Note 21

cry		

Look at your words.
Circle the words that belong
to the same word family as **cry**.

Learn to spell one of these words, and
you will be able to spell
all of the words.

Say this word: **thank**

Think of words that rhyme.
Write the words.
Your teacher will help you with the spelling.

Note 22

thank		

Look at your words.
Circle the words that belong
to the same word family as **thank**.

Learn to spell one of these words, and
you will be able to spell
all of the words.

Divide and conquer.

How can you divide and conquer these words?

boxes   _____
notice   _____
carry   _____

Divide and conquer

Do you see
- ❏ **common beginning parts?**
- ❏ **common end parts?**
- ❏ **little words?**

Use a spelling rule.

Practice the *Doubling* rule.

Say the base word.
Add the end part to the base word.
Say the new word.

gas + ed   _____
gas + ing   _____
gas + y   _____
lug + ed   _____
lug + ing   _____
lug + s   _____
box + ed   _____
box + ing   _____
box + er   _____
box + s   _____
car + y   _____

Doubling rule

If a word has ONE syllable and ends with ONE vowel and ONE consonant, double the final consonant when you add an end part that starts with a vowel.

Practice the *Y* rule (part 1).

Say the word.
Divide the word into two syllables.
Underline the letter that makes
the long **e** sound.

Y rule (part 1)

When you hear the *long e* sound at the end of a word that has two syllables, use *y*.

You have a good chance of being right.

carry

Practice the *Y* rule (part 2).

Say the base word.
Add the end part to the base word.
Say the new word.

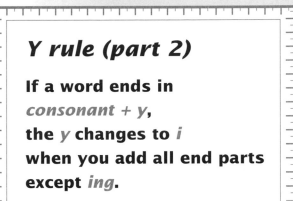

Y rule (part 2)

If a word ends in
consonant + y,
the *y* changes to *i*
when you add all end parts
except *ing*.

carry + s*	_____
carry + er	_____
carry + ed	_____
carry + ing	_____
cry + ing	_____
cry + ed	_____
cry + s*	_____
cry + er	_____

* Change the **y** to **i** and add **es**.
You always need to add **es**
—not only **s**— so that the word
sounds right.

Practice the *Drop the E* rule.

Say the base word.
Add the end part to the base word.
Say the new word.

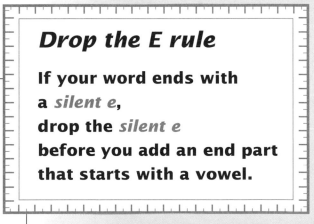

Drop the E rule

If your word ends with
a *silent e*,
drop the *silent e*
before you add an end part
that starts with a vowel.

notice + ed	_____
notice + ing	_____
notice + s	_____
move + ed	_____
move + ing	_____
move + er	_____
move + s	_____

Look for tricky parts.

Look at the words below.
Look for the tricky parts.
Use the six steps to help you spell the words.

month	_____
one	_____
heat	_____
move	_____
you	_____
notice	_____

Remember to . . .

1. **Read the word slowly.**
2. **Mark any tricky part.**
3. **Study the tricky part.**
4. **Cover the word.**
5. **Write the word.**
6. **Check the spelling.**

Trying out your spelling tools

1 — Your teacher will read a letter.
Listen. Finish the letter.

Note 23

Use your spelling tools.

Say, listen, and write.

Make a word family.

Divide and conquer.

Use a spelling rule.

Look for tricky parts.

Hi Sis,
I need your help! ① We want to
_____ this _____. ② I have
_____ week to _____
a place. ③ I _____ to _____ for a place with more
_____. ④ I'm going to have to _____ and
_____ tons of _____. ⑤ I want to _____.
Help! ⑥ Do you have time to fly down and help us _____?

⑦ I gave_____ to the landlord last week. ⑧ They are still
_____ the furnace. ⑨ There is no _____ and no
_____!

⑩ I have to get out of this _____! ⑪ Let me know if you can
come. _____ you.

Deb

2— Check your spelling.
Your teacher will help you.

Which words gave you trouble?
Use a different spelling tool.
Try again.

3— Your teacher will read another letter.
You are going to spell new words.
This will give you a chance
to try out your spelling tools.

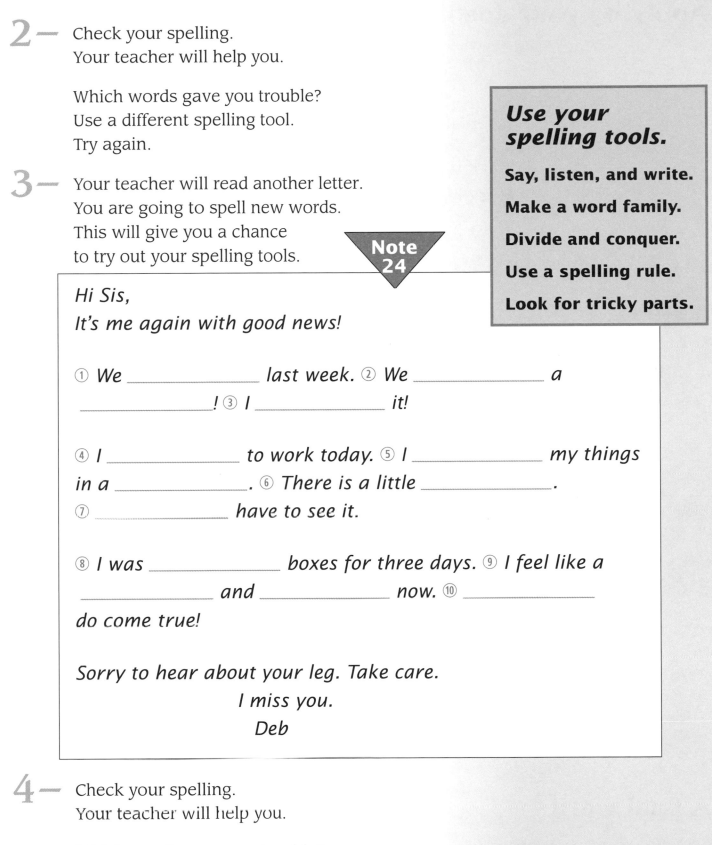

Note 24

Use your spelling tools.

Say, listen, and write.

Make a word family.

Divide and conquer.

Use a spelling rule.

Look for tricky parts.

Hi Sis,
It's me again with good news!

① *We _____ last week.* ② *We _____ a*
_____*!* ③ *I _____ it!*

④ *I _____ to work today.* ⑤ *I _____ my things*
in a _____. ⑥ *There is a little _____.*
⑦ _____ *have to see it.*

⑧ *I was _____ boxes for three days.* ⑨ *I feel like a*
_____ *and _____ now.* ⑩ _____
do come true!

Sorry to hear about your leg. Take care.
I miss you.
Deb

4— Check your spelling.
Your teacher will help you.

Which words gave you trouble?
Use a different spelling tool.
Try again.

Applying your spelling tools

1— Look at this example.

Jack is going to move.
He gives his landlord notice.

July 21

I will be moving next month.

Thank you.

Sincerely,
Jack Keens
Jack Keens
Apt. 28

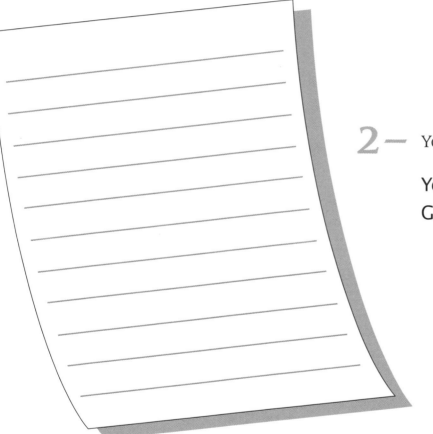

2— Your turn.

You are moving.
Give your landlord notice.

A final word

Which words about **changes**
would you like to add
to your dictionary?

Practice words

sports	baseball	skate	classes	swimming
kick	show	town	shops	bikes
fishing	bus	bowling	summer	winter

Working with spelling tools

Say, listen, and write.

Say each word.
Listen to each sound.
Write the word as you say it.

sport	_____	fishing	_____	shops	_____
bus	_____	winter	_____	swim	_____

If you say these words slowly,
you will have a good chance
of spelling them right.

Make a word family.

Say this word: **kick**

Think of words that rhyme.
Write the words.
Your teacher will help you with the spelling.

Note
25

kick

Look at your words.
Circle the words that belong to the same word family as **kick**.

Learn to spell one of these words, and
you will be able to spell
all of the words.

Say this word: **show**

Think of words that rhyme.
Write the words.
Your teacher will help you with the spelling.

Note
26

show

Look at your words.
Circle the words that belong to the same word family as **show**.

Learn to spell one of these words, and
you will be able to spell
all of the words.

Say this word: **town**

Think of words that rhyme.
Write the words.
Your teacher will help you with the spelling.

Note
27

town

Look at your words.
Circle the words that belong
to the same word family as **town**.

Learn to spell one of these words, and
you will be able to spell
all of the words.

Say this word: **bike**

Think of words that rhyme.
Write the words.
Your teacher will help you with the spelling.

Note
28

bike

Look at your words.
Circle the words that belong
to the same word family as **bike**.

Learn to spell one of these words, and
you will be able to spell
all of the words.

Divide and conquer.

How can you divide and conquer these words?

sports _____
classes _____
bikes _____
bowling _____
baseball _____
fishing _____
shops _____

Divide and conquer

Do you see
- ❏ common beginning parts?
- ❏ common end parts?
- ❏ little words?

Use a spelling rule.

Practice the *Doubling* rule.

Say the base word.
Add the end part to the base word.
Say the new word.

swim + ing   *swimming*
swim + er _____
swim + s _____
bus + ed _____
bus + ing _____
sum + er _____
shop + ed _____
shop + ing _____
shop + er _____
shop + s _____

Doubling rule

If a word has ONE syllable and ends with ONE vowel and ONE consonant, double the final consonant when you add an end part that starts with a vowel.

Practice the *Silent E* rule.

Say the word.
Underline the long vowel sound.
Circle the silent **e**.

bike	skate	base

Practice the *Drop the E* rule.

Say the base word.
Add the end part to the base word.
Say the new word.

bike   + ed   _____
bike   + ing   _____
bike   + s   _____
bike   + er   _____
skate + ing   _____
skate + s   _____
skate + ed   _____
base + ing   _____
base + s   _____
base + ed   _____

Look for tricky parts.

Look at the words below.
Look for the tricky parts.
Use the six steps to help you
spell the words.

class	_____
bowl	_____
ball	_____

Remember to...

1. **Read the word slowly.**
2. **Mark any tricky part.**
3. **Study the tricky part.**
4. **Cover the word.**
5. **Write the word.**
6. **Check the spelling.**

Trying out your spelling tools

1— Your teacher will read a passage.
Listen.
Finish the ideas.

There was always something to do when I was a kid.

① In the _____ , we played

_____ or _____-the-can.

② We rode our _____ all the time.

③ We had _____ _____.

④ We played all kinds of _____.

⑤ The best of all was _____ in the pond. ⑥ In the _____ we would _____ on the pond. ⑦ Sometimes, we took the _____ to _____.

⑧ We went _____ or to a _____.

⑨ We looked in the _____ windows.

Things have changed a lot!

Use your spelling tools.

Say, listen, and write.

Make a word family.

Divide and conquer.

Use a spelling rule.

Look for tricky parts.

2— Check your spelling.
Your teacher will help you.

Which words gave you trouble?
Use a different spelling tool.
Try again.

3 — Your teacher will read another passage.
You are going to spell new words.
This will give you a chance
to try out your spelling tools.

Note 30

① Kids don't play _____- up baseball. ② _____ is not cool. ③ _____ spend a lot of time in _____ malls. ④ _____ cost a _____ of money. ⑤ _____ is not _____ at night. ⑥ What _____ kids _____?

Use your spelling tools

Say, listen, and write.

Make a word family.

Divide and conquer.

Use a spelling rule.

Look for tricky parts.

4 — Check your spelling.
Your teacher will help you.

Which words gave you trouble?
Use a different spelling tool.
Try again.

Applying the spelling tools

1 — Look at this example.

Kate wants to put an ad
in the personals.

Here is a list of what she likes to do.

Take long walks
Go for long bike rides
Sit and dream
by the lake
Watch funny movies

2— Your turn.

What do you like to do?

Write an ad for the personals.

I like to . . .

A final word

Which words about **things to do** would you like to add to your dictionary?

bankrupt

Italian moneylenders used to do business on a small bench. They had to break up their bench if their business failed. The Latin way to say *broken bench* is *banca rupta*. Later, *banca rupta* became *bankrupt* in English.

unit 8

community
Action

Practice words

need	vote	hall	help	rally
plan	donate	drive	food	phone
meet	city	busy	sale	door

Working with spelling tools

Say, listen, and write.

Say each word.
Listen to each sound.
Write the word as you say it.

help _____   plan _____

If you say these words slowly,
you will have a good chance
of spelling them right.

Make a word family.

Say this word: **hall**

Think of words that rhyme.
Write the words.
Your teacher will help you with the spelling.

Note 31

hall _____ _____ _____

_____ _____ _____

_____ _____ _____

_____ _____ _____

_____ _____ _____

Look at your words.
Circle the words that belong to the same word family as **hall**.

Learn to spell one of these words, and
you will be able to spell
all of the words.

Say this word: **meet**

Think of words that rhyme.
Write the words.
Your teacher will help you with the spelling.

Note 32

meet _____ _____ _____

_____ _____ _____

_____ _____ _____

_____ _____ _____

_____ _____ _____

Look at your words.
Circle the words that belong to the same word family as **meet**.

Learn to spell one of these words, and
you will be able to spell
all of the words.

The Spelling Toolbox ■ **Workbook 1**

Say this word: **need**

Think of words that rhyme.
Write the words.
Your teacher will help you with the spelling.

Note
33

need		

Look at your words.
Circle the words that belong to the same word family as **need**.

Learn to spell one of these words, and
you will be able to spell
all of the words.

✂ Divide and conquer.

How can you divide and conquer
these words?

donate	_____
door	_____

Divide and conquer

Do you see
❏ **common beginning parts?**
❏ **common end parts?**
❏ **little words?**

hunky-dory

In 1868, there was a breath freshener.
It was called *Hunkidori*.
People started to say *Hunkidori* a lot.
Today, *hunky-dory* means everything is okay.

Use a spelling rule.

Practice the *Doubling* rule.

Say the base word.
Add the end part to the base word.
Say the new word.

plan + ing	planning
plan + ed	_____
plan + s	_____
plan + er	_____

> ## Doubling rule
>
> **If a word has ONE syllable and ends with ONE vowel and ONE consonant, double the final consonant when you add an end part that starts with a vowel.**

Practice the *Y* rule (part 1).

Say the word.
Divide the word into two syllables.
Underline the letter
that makes the long **e** sound.

busy	_____
rally	_____
city	_____

> ## Y rule (part 1)
>
> **When you hear the *long e* sound at the end of a word that has two syllables, use *y*.**
>
> **You have a good chance of being right.**

Practice the *Y* rule (part 2).

Say the base word.
Add the end part to the base word.
Say the new word.

busy + er	_____
rally + ed	_____
rally + ing	_____
rally + s	_____
city + s	_____

> ## Y rule (part 2)
>
> **If a word ends in *consonant + y*, the *y* changes to *i* when you add all end parts except *ing*.**

Practice the *Silent E* rule.

Say the word.
Underline the long vowel sound.
Circle the silent **e**.

donate	phone	vote
drive	sale	

Practice the *Drop the E* rule.

Say the base word.
Add the end part to the base word.
Say the new word.

donate + ed   _____
donate + ing   _____
donate + s   _____
donate + er   _____
phone + ing   _____
phone + ed   _____
phone + s   _____
vote   + ed   _____
vote   + ing   _____
vote   + s   _____
vote   + er   _____
drive + er   _____
drive + ing   _____
drive + s   _____
sale   + s   _____

Look for tricky parts.

Look at the word below.
Look for the tricky part.
Use the six steps to help you spell the word.

food _____

Remember to...

1. **Read the word slowly.**
2. **Mark any tricky part.**
3. **Study the tricky part.**
4. **Cover the word.**
5. **Write the word.**
6. **Check the spelling.**

Trying out your spelling tools

1— Your teacher will read a notice from a newsletter.
Listen.
Finish the notice.

Note 34

① We know you are _____. ② But,
we _____ your _____.
③ The _____ is to _____ for
a _____. ④ We will meet at
_____ _____.

⑤ The Pizza Place will _____
_____. ⑥ Drinks will be on
_____. ⑦ You may win a
_____ prize!

⑧ _____ us _____ out
crime! ⑨ _____: 888-Fight.

Use your spelling tools.

Say, listen, and write.

Make a word family.

Divide and conquer.

Use a spelling rule.

Look for tricky parts.

2— Check your spelling.
Your teacher will help you.

Which words gave you trouble?
Use a different spelling tool.
Try again.

3— Your teacher will read a letter.
You are going to spell new words.
This will give you a chance
to try out your spelling tools.

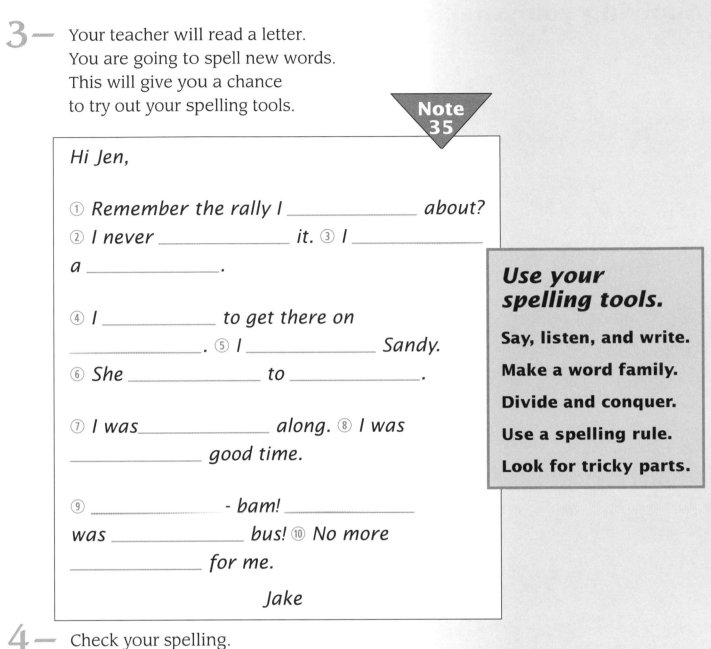

Note 35

Hi Jen,

① Remember the rally I _____ about?
② I never _____ it. ③ I _____
a _____ .

④ I _____ to get there on
_____ . ⑤ I _____ Sandy.
⑥ She _____ to _____ .

⑦ I was_____ along. ⑧ I was
_____ good time.

⑨ _____ - bam! _____
was _____ bus! ⑩ No more
_____ for me.

Jake

Use your spelling tools.

Say, listen, and write.

Make a word family.

Divide and conquer.

Use a spelling rule.

Look for tricky parts.

4— Check your spelling.
Your teacher will help you.

Which words gave you trouble?
Use a different spelling tool.
Try again.

Applying your spelling tools

1 — Look at this example.

Here is a poster.
It is asking for your help.

2 — Your turn.

Who needs help in your community?

Make a poster.

A final word

Which words about **community action**
would you like to add to your dictionary?

Practice words

school	block	cop	teach	people
church	club	reach	care	pals
buddy	take	know	hi	nice

Working with spelling tools

Say, listen, and write.

Say each word.
Listen to each sound.
Write the word as you say it.

club	_____	pals	_____
cop	_____	hi	_____

If you say these words slowly,
you will have a good chance
of spelling them right.

Make a word family.

Say this word: **block**

Think of words that rhyme.
Write the words.
Your teacher will help you with the spelling.

Note
36

block _____ _____
_____ _____ _____
_____ _____ _____
_____ _____ _____

Look at your words.
Circle the words that belong to the same word family as **block**.

Learn to spell one of these words, and
you will be able to spell
all of the words.

Say this word: **take**

Think of words that rhyme.
Write the words.
Your teacher will help you with the spelling.

Note
37

take _____ _____
_____ _____ _____
_____ _____ _____
_____ _____ _____

Look at your words.
Circle the words that belong to the same word family as **take**.

Learn to spell one of these words, and
you will be able to spell
all of the words.

Say this word: **nice**

Think of words that rhyme.
Write the words.
Your teacher will help you with the spelling.

Note 38

nice _____ _____

_____ _____ _____

_____ _____ _____

Look at your words.
Circle the words that belong to the same word family as **nice**.

Learn to spell one of these words, and
you will be able to spell
all of the words.

Divide and conquer.

How can you divide and conquer
these words?

teach _____

reach _____

pals _____

know _____

Divide and conquer
Do you see
❑ **common beginning parts?**
❑ **common end parts?**
❑ **little words?**

fall in love

Five hundred years ago
a romantic man wrote this line:
"So fare I-falling into love's dance."
Now we just say *falling in love*.

Use a spelling rule.

Practice the *Doubling* rule.

Say the base word.
Add the end part to the base word.
Say the new word.

club + ing	_____
club + ed	_____
club + s	_____
pal + s	_____
cop + er	_____
cop + s	_____
bud + ing	_____
bud + y	_____

Doubling rule

If a word has ONE syllable and ends with ONE vowel and ONE consonant, double the final consonant when you add an end part that starts with a vowel.

Practice the *Y* rule (part 1).

Say the word.
Divide the word into two syllables.
Underline the letter
that makes the long **e** sound.

buddy	_____

Y rule (part 1)

**When you hear
the *long e* sound
at the end of a word
that has two syllables,
use *y*.**

**You have a good chance
of being right.**

Practice the *Y* rule (part 2).

Say the base word.
Add the end part to the base word.
Say the new word.

buddy + s	_____

* Change the **y** to **i** and add **es**.
  You always need to add **es**—not only **s**—
  so that the word sounds right.

Y rule (part 2)

**If a word ends in
consonant + y,
the *y* changes to *i*
when you add all end parts
except *ing*.**

Practice the *Silent E* rule.

Say the word.
Underline the long vowel sound.
Circle the silent **e**.

take	nice	care

Silent E rule

When you add the letter *e* to the end of a word, the short vowel sound in that word changes to a long vowel sound.

Practice the *Drop the E* rule.

Say the base word.
Add the end part to the base word.
Say the new word.

take + ing _____
take + s _____
take + er _____
care + ing _____
care + ed _____
care + s _____

Drop the E rule

If your word ends with a *silent e*, drop the *silent e* before you add an end part that starts with a vowel.

Look for tricky parts.

Look at the words below.
Look for the tricky parts.
Use the six steps to help you spell the words.

school _____
people _____
church _____
know _____
reach _____
teach _____

Remember to...

1. **Read the word slowly.**
2. **Mark any tricky part.**
3. **Study the tricky part.**
4. **Cover the word.**
5. **Write the word.**
6. **Check the spelling.**

Trying out your spelling tools

1—
Your teacher will read a letter.
Listen.
Finish the letter.

Note 39

① _____ Jane,

② I *go to a* _____ *now.* ③ *It's down the* _____ .

④ *I* _____ *a lot of* _____ *there.* ⑤ *It's in the* _____ *basement.*

⑥ *I have a lot of* _____ _____ . ⑦ *They* _____ *me a lot.* ⑧ *It's like* _____ . ⑨ *One* _____ *is a* _____ *of mine.* ⑩ *It's good to* _____ *out to people.*

⑪ _____ _____ ,
Dad

Use your spelling tools.

Say, listen, and write.

Make a word family.

Divide and conquer.

Use a spelling rule.

Look for tricky parts.

2—
Check your spelling.
Your teacher will help you.

Which words gave you trouble?
Use a different spelling tool.
Try again.

3—
Your teacher will read another letter.
You are going to spell new words.
This will give you a chance to try out your spelling tools.

Hi Dad,

① I'm _____ you have new

_____. ② You seem _____.

③ I'm _____ care of my neighbour's

_____. ④ My neighbour

_____to _____her

boyfriend.

⑤ The dog's name is _____. ⑥ He

_____ my neighbour _____

away. ⑦ He gets _____ every day.

⑧ We'll both be happy _____ she

_____ home.

⑨ See _____,

Jane

Use your spelling tools.

Say, listen, and write.

Make a word family.

Divide and conquer.

Use a spelling rule.

Look for tricky parts.

4— Check your spelling.
Your teacher will help you.

Which words gave you trouble?
Use a different spelling tool.
Try again.

Applying your spelling tools

1— Look at this example.

Here is a notice
from a newsletter.

Come to the Scrapbook Club

We meet every Monday night.
Time: 7:00 to 9:00
Place: St. Mary's School Basement

See you there!

2— Your turn.

What club would you like to start?
Write a notice.

A final word

Which words about **community relations**
would you like to add
to your dictionary?

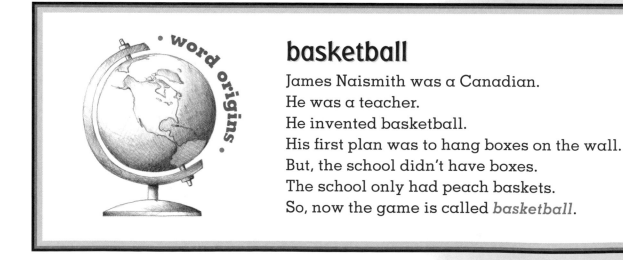

basketball

James Naismith was a Canadian.
He was a teacher.
He invented basketball.
His first plan was to hang boxes on the wall.
But, the school didn't have boxes.
The school only had peach baskets.
So, now the game is called *basketball*.

Practice words

shut	build	clear	wider	pave
plant	prices	empty	lot	shrubs
put	new	lights	road	street

Working with spelling tools

Say, listen, and write.

Say each word.
Listen to each sound.
Write the word as you say it.

shut _____	wider _____	shrub _____
plant _____	lot _____	

If you say these words slowly,
you will have a good chance
of spelling them right.

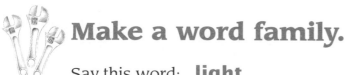

Make a word family.

Say this word: **light**

Think of words that rhyme.
Write the words.
Your teacher will help you with the spelling.

**Note
41**

light _____   _____

_____   _____   _____

_____   _____   _____

_____   _____   _____

Look at your words.
Circle the words that belong to the same word family as **light**.

Learn to spell one of these words, and
you will be able to spell
all of the words.

Say this word: **clear**

Think of words that rhyme.
Write the words.
Your teacher will help you with the spelling.

**Note
42**

clear _____   _____

_____   _____   _____

_____   _____   _____

_____   _____   _____

Look at your words.
Circle the words that belong to the same word family as **clear**.

Learn to spell one of these words, and
you will be able to spell
all of the words.

Divide and conquer.

How can you divide and conquer these words?

prices _____

shrubs _____

lights _____

lots _____

Use a spelling rule.

Practice the *Doubling* rule.

Say the base word.
Add the end part to the base word.
Say the new word.

shut + ing _____

shut + s _____

put + s _____

put + ing _____

Doubling rule

If a word has ONE syllable and ends with ONE vowel and ONE consonant, double the final consonant when you add an end part that starts with a vowel.

Practice the *Y* rule (part 1).

Say the word.
Divide the word into two syllables.
Underline the letter
that makes the long **e** sound.

empty _____

Y rule (part 1)

When you hear
the *long e* sound
at the end of a word
that has two syllables,
use *y*.

You have a good chance
of being right.

Practice the *Y* rule (part 2).

Say the base word.
Add the end part to the base word.
Say the new word.

empty + er _____

empty + ed _____

empty + ing _____

empty + s _____

> ## Y rule (part 2)
>
> **If a word ends in
> *consonant + y*,
> the *y* changes to *i*
> when you add all end parts
> except *ing*.**

Practice the *Silent E* rule.

Say the word.
Underline the long vowel sound.
Circle the silent **e**.

wide   price   pave

> ## Silent E rule
>
> **When you add the letter *e*
> to the end of a word,
> the short vowel sound
> in that word changes to
> a long vowel sound.**

Practice the *Drop the E* rule.

Say the base word.
Add the end part to the base word.
Say the new word.

wide + er _____

price + ing _____

price + s _____

price + ed _____

pave + ed _____

pave + s _____

pave + ing _____

> ## Drop the E rule
>
> **If your word ends with
> a *silent e*,
> drop the *silent e*
> before you add an end part
> that starts with a vowel.**

Look for tricky parts.

Look at the words below.
Look for the tricky parts.
Use the six steps to help you
spell the words.

new	_____
street	_____
road	_____
build	_____
put	_____
clear	_____

Remember to . . .

1. **Read the word slowly.**

2. **Mark any tricky part.**

3. **Study the tricky part.**

4. **Cover the word.**

5. **Write the word.**

6. **Check the spelling.**

Trying out your spelling tools

1— Your teacher will read a letter. Listen.
Finish the letter.

Note 43

Use your spelling tools.

Say, listen, and write.

Make a word family.

Divide and conquer.

Use a spelling rule.

Look for tricky parts.

Dear Mayor:

Our area looks bad! We need to . . .

① ■ _____ out the _____
   _____ .

② ■ _____ down the bars.

③ ■ _____ up _____
   _____ signs and _____ .

④ ■ _____ more trees and
   _____ .

⑤ ■ _____ the _____ .

⑥ ■ Make the roads _____ .

⑦ ■ _____ a rec centre.

⑧ Then let's watch our land _____ go up!

Tim Dakin

2— Check your spelling.
Your teacher will help you.

Which words gave you trouble?
Use a different spelling tool.
Try again.

3— Your teacher will read another letter.
You are going to spell new words.
This will give you a chance
to try out your spelling tools.

Note 44

Dear Tim Daken:

① We don't need more _____.
② We don't need more _____.
③ We need to think in the _____ way.

④ _____ roads is _____.
⑤ _____ streets wider is
_____. ⑥ _____ we need
_____ community _____.
⑦ _____ starts _____
_____ people first!

Lin Yung

Use your spelling tools.

Say, listen, and write.

Make a word family.

Divide and conquer.

Use a spelling rule.

Look for tricky parts.

4— Check your spelling.
Your teacher will help you.

Which words gave you trouble?
Use a different spelling tool.
Try again.

Applying your spelling tools

1— Look at this example.

Some people want to see changes.
Here is their letter.

To the Mayor:

We would like
- more bus service
- safer streets
- more night life

Signed
The people of
Upper Hills Community

2— Your turn.

What changes would you like to see
in your community?

Write a letter to the mayor.

Dear Mayor:

I would like to see . . .

- _____
- _____
- _____
- _____
- _____
- _____

Yours truly,

A final word

Which words about **community changes**
would you like to add
to your dictionary?

Practice words

St.	Rd.	Apt.	skills	learn
things	March	April	Jan.	work
job	finish	start	try	like

Working with spelling tools

Say, listen, and write.

Say each word.
Listen to each sound.
Write the word as you say it.

start _____	job _____	thing _____
finish _____	March _____	

If you say these words slowly,
you will have a good chance
of spelling them right.

Make a word family.

Say this word: **skill**

Think of words that rhyme.
Write the words.
Your teacher will help you with the spelling.

Note 45

_____ skill _____   _____   _____

_____   _____   _____

_____   _____   _____

_____   _____   _____

Look at your words.
Circle the words that belong to the same word family as **skill**.

Learn to spell one of these words, and
you will be able to spell
all of the words.

Say this word: **try**

Think of words that rhyme.
Write the words.
Your teacher will help you with the spelling.

Note 46

_____ try _____   _____

_____   _____   _____

_____   _____   _____

_____   _____   _____

Look at your words.
Circle the words that belong to the same word family as **try**.

Learn to spell one of these words, and
you will be able to spell
all of the words.

Say this word: **like**

Think of words that rhyme.
Write the words.
Your teacher will help you with the spelling.

Note
47

__like__ _____ _____

_____ _____ _____

_____ _____

Look at your words.
Circle the words that belong
to the same word family as **like**.

Learn to spell one of these words, and
you will be able to spell
all of the words.

Divide and conquer.

How can you divide and conquer
these words?

skills _____

learn _____

things _____

Divide and conquer.

Do you see
❏ **common beginning parts?**
❏ **common end parts?**
❏ **little words?**

· word origins ·

blow the whistle

Referees use whistles.
They blow the whistles
when a player does something wrong.
Now, *blow the whistle* means
to *tell on someone*.

Use a spelling rule.

Practice the *Y* rule (part 2).

Say the base word.
Add the end part to the base word.
Say the new word.

try + ed	_____
try + ing	_____
try + s	_____

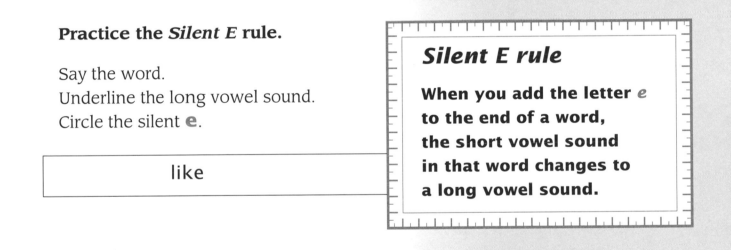

Y rule (part 2)

**If a word ends in
consonant + y,
the *y* changes to *i*
when you add all end parts
except *ing*.**

Practice the *Silent E* rule.

Say the word.
Underline the long vowel sound.
Circle the silent **e**.

like

Silent E rule

**When you add the letter *e*
to the end of a word,
the short vowel sound
in that word changes to
a long vowel sound.**

Practice the *Drop the E* rule.

Say the base word.
Add the end part to the base word.
Say the new word.

like + ed	_____
like + ing	_____
like + s	_____

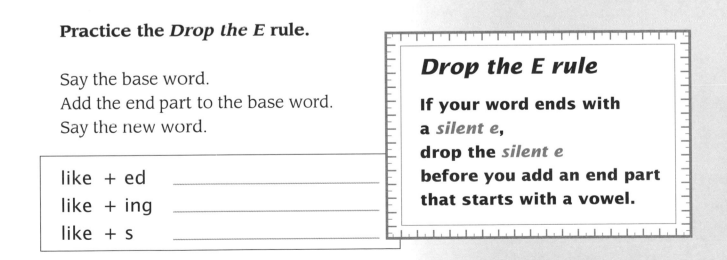

Drop the E rule

**If your word ends with
a *silent e*,
drop the *silent e*
before you add an end part
that starts with a vowel.**

Look for tricky parts.

Look at the words below.
Look for the tricky parts.
Use the six steps to help you
spell the words.

St. _____

Rd. _____

Apt. _____

April _____

Jan. _____

work _____

Remember to...

1. **Read the word slowly.**
2. **Mark any tricky part.**
3. **Study the tricky part.**
4. **Cover the word.**
5. **Write the word.**
6. **Check the spelling.**

Trying out your spelling tools

1 — Your teacher will read some information.
Listen.
Finish the ideas.

Note 48

① Address: 25 Main _____ /_____ 14

② Contact: 113 Haven_____

③ Birthdate: _____ 9, 1960

④ I have computer _____.

⑤ I _____ well with people.

⑥ I _____ to _____ new
_____.

⑦ I _____ fast on the _____.

⑧ _____ : _____ 2000

⑨ _____ : _____ 2000

Use your spelling tools.

Say, listen, and write.

Make a word family.

Divide and conquer.

Use a spelling rule.

Look for tricky parts.

2— Check your spelling.
Your teacher will help you.

Which words gave you trouble?
Use a different spelling tool.
Try again.

3— Your teacher will read more information.
You are going to spell new words.
This will give you a chance
to try out your spelling tools.

Note 49

① I'm a fast _____.

② I have good _____ skills.

③ I have _____ _____
computer _____.

④ I _____ _____ high
school.

⑤ I'm _____ to find a _____
job.

⑥ I'm a _____ _____.

⑦ I know _____.

⑧ I like _____ and _____
_____.

Use your spelling tools.

Say, listen, and write.

Make a word family.

Divide and conquer.

Use a spelling rule.

Look for tricky parts.

4— Check your spelling.
Your teacher will help you.

Which words gave you trouble?
Use a different spelling tool.
Try again.

Applying your spelling tools

1 — Look at this example.

Mike is looking for a job.
Here is his form.

How could Mike
improve his application?

Application for Employment

Name   Mike Troy

Address   820 Nells Rd. Apt. 4

Education

St. James High School (finished 2000)

Niagara college (finished 2002)

Work Experience

Hobbies/Skills/Interests

Working on my car.

Watching T.V.

honey

Do you call someone you love *honey*?
The Greeks did the same thing a long time ago.
There is a ring in a British museum.
The ring is a Greek wedding ring.
The ring is thousands of years old.
There is a Greek word on the ring.
The word is *meli*.
Meli is Greek for *honey*.

2 — Look at this example.   You need a job.
Fill in the form.

Application for Employment

Name _____

Address _____

_____

Birthdate _____

Education
_____
_____
_____

Work Experience
_____
_____
_____
_____
_____

Hobbies/Skills/Interests
_____
_____
_____
_____

A final word

Which words about **work forms**
would you like to add
to your dictionary?

unit
12

work

Routines

Practice words

sign	break	always	never	morning
noon	shift	day	laugh	joke
soup	faces	snack	lunch	play

Working with spelling tools

Say, listen, and write.

Say each word.
Listen to each sound.
Write the word as you say it.

shift _____	morning _____
never _____	lunch _____

If you say these words slowly,
you will have a good chance
of spelling them right.

Make a word family.

Say this word: **noon**

Think of words that rhyme.
Write the words.
Your teacher will help you with the spelling.

Note 50

noon	_____	_____
_____	_____	_____

Look at your words.
Circle the words that belong
to the same word family as **noon**.

Learn to spell one of these words, and
you will be able to spell
all of the words.

Say this word: **snack**

Think of words that rhyme.
Write the words.
Your teacher will help you with the spelling.

Note 51

snack	_____	_____
_____	_____	_____

Look at your words.
Circle the words that belong
to the same word family as **snack**.

Learn to spell one of these words, and
you will be able to spell
all of the words.

Say these words: **day**   **play**

Think of words that rhyme.
Write the words.
Your teacher will help you with the spelling.

Note 52

day
play
_____ _____ _____
_____ _____ _____
_____ _____ _____
_____ _____ _____

Look at your words.
Circle the words that belong to the same word family as **day** and **play**.

Learn to spell one of these words, and
you will be able to spell
all of the words.

Say this word: **face**

Think of words that rhyme.
Write the words.
Your teacher will help you with the spelling.

Note 53

face
_____ _____ _____
_____ _____ _____
_____ _____ _____
_____ _____ _____

Look at your words.
Circle the words that belong to the same word family as **face**.

Learn to spell one of these words, and
you will be able to spell
all of the words.

Divide and conquer.

How can you divide and conquer these words?

always _____

faces _____

never _____

Use a spelling rule.

Practice the *Silent E* rule.

Say the word.
Underline the long vowel sound.
Circle the silent **e**.

joke   face

Practice the *Drop the E* rule.

Say the base word.
Add the end part to the base word.
Say the new word.

joke + ed _____
joke + ing _____
joke + er _____
joke + s _____
face + ing _____
face + ed _____
face + s _____

Look for tricky parts.

Look at the words below.
Look for the tricky parts.
Use the six steps to help you
spell the words.

sign   _____
break   _____
soup   _____
laugh   _____

Remember to...

1. **Read the word slowly.**
2. **Mark any tricky part.**
3. **Study the tricky part.**
4. **Cover the word.**
5. **Write the word.**
6. **Check the spelling.**

Trying out your spelling tools

1— Your teacher will read a passage.
Listen.
Finish the ideas.

Note 54

① I have the _____ _____
at a doughnut shop. ② We _____
have to _____ in or out. ③ I have
a _____ every hour. ④ I have
_____ at _____ for
_____. ⑤ I'll have a doughnut
_____ later.

⑥ I see the same _____ every
_____. ⑦ We _____
_____ and _____. ⑧ We
_____ tricks on each other.

I like the routine. It makes me feel safe.

Use your spelling tools.

Say, listen, and write.

Make a word family.

Divide and conquer.

Use a spelling rule.

Look for tricky parts.

2 — Check your spelling.
Your teacher will help you.

Which words gave you trouble?
Use a different spelling tool.
Try again.

3 — Your teacher will read another passage.
You are going to spell new words.
This will give you a chance
to try out your spelling tools.

Note 55

① I _____ the _____ shift.
② We get a _____-minute break every
_____ hours. ③ _____,
I sneak a _____.

④ _____ is no time for _____
around. ⑤ The cars on the _____
keep going _____. ⑥ _____
never stop. ⑦ No time _____.
⑧ It's like _____ long _____.
⑨ _____ job is _____ me.

Use your spelling tools.

Say, listen, and write.

Make a word family.

Divide and conquer.

Use a spelling rule.

Look for tricky parts.

4 — Check your spelling.
Your teacher will help you.

Which words gave you trouble?
Use a different spelling tool.
Try again.

Applying your spelling tools

1— Look at this example.

Fatima wants a new job.
This is her wish list.

I would like to...
— eat lunch in a quiet room.
— drink coffee when I want
— have afternoons off
on sunny days
— always be with my kids
at night
— never work midnights

2— Your turn.

Think about the perfect job.
What is your wish list?

I wish I had a job
where I could . . .

A final word

Which words about **work routines** would you like to add to your dictionary?

Practice words

wanted	buy	sell	offer	give
free	cheap	away	shape	found
lost	used	ride	toy	best

Working with spelling tools

Say, listen, and write.

Say each word.
Listen to each sound.
Write the word as you say it.

lost	_____ best	_____

If you say these words slowly,
you will have a good chance
of spelling them right.

Make a word family.

Say this word: **sell**

Think of words that rhyme.
Write the words.
Your teacher will help you with the spelling.

Note 56

sell		

Look at your words.
Circle the words that belong
to the same word family as **sell**.

Learn to spell one of these words, and
you will be able to spell
all of the words.

Say this word: **found**

Think of words that rhyme.
Write the words.
Your teacher will help you with the spelling.

Note 57

found		

Look at your words.
Circle the words that belong
to the same word family as **found**.

Learn to spell one of these words, and
you will be able to spell
all of the words.

Say this word: **toy**

Think of words that rhyme.
Write the words.
Your teacher will help you with the spelling.

Note 58

toy _____ _____
_____ _____ _____
_____ _____ _____

Look at your words.
Circle the words that belong
to the same word family as **toy**.

Learn to spell one of these words, and
you will be able to spell
all of the words.

Divide and conquer.

How can you divide and conquer
these words?

wanted   _____
offer   _____
away   _____

Divide and conquer

Do you see
❑ **common beginning parts?**
❑ **common end parts?**
❑ **little words?**

· word origins ·

Flea market

Dutch people settled in New York many years ago.
They had a market called _Valley Market_.
The name _Valley Market_ became _Vlie Market_.
The name _Vlie Market_ then became _flea market_.

Use a spelling rule.

Practice the *Silent E* rule.

Say the word.
Underline the long vowel sound.
Circle the silent **e**.

ride	shape	use

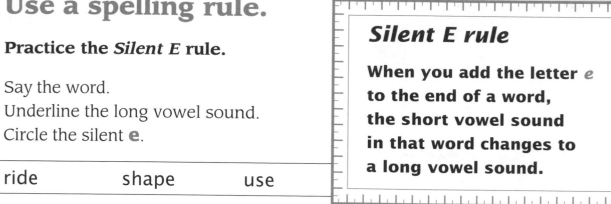

Silent E rule

When you add the letter *e*
to the end of a word,
the short vowel sound
in that word changes to
a long vowel sound.

Practice the *Drop the E* rule.

Say the base word.
Add the end part to the base word.
Say the new word.

ride + ing _____

ride + s _____

ride + er _____

give + er _____

give + s _____

shape + ed _____

shape + ing _____

shape + s _____

use + er _____

use + ed _____

use + ing _____

use + s _____

Drop the E rule

If your word ends with
a *silent e*,
drop the *silent e*
before you add an end part
that starts with a vowel.

Look for tricky parts.

Look at the words below.
Look for the tricky parts.
Use the six steps to help you
spell the words.

cheap	_____
buy	_____
free	_____
give	_____

Remember to . . .

1. **Read the word slowly.**
2. **Mark any tricky part.**
3. **Study the tricky part.**
4. **Cover the word.**
5. **Write the word.**
6. **Check the spelling.**

Trying out your spelling tools

1 — Your teacher will read some items from ads.
Listen.
Finish the items.

Note 59

① _____ car for sale
② _____ and _____
③ _____ to a good home
④ _____ _____
⑤ Child's _____ to _____
_____
⑥ _____ and in good _____
⑦ We _____ and _____
⑧ _____ : _____ to work

Use your spelling tools.

Say, listen, and write.

Make a word family.

Divide and conquer.

Use a spelling rule.

Look for tricky parts.

2 — Check your spelling.
Your teacher will help you.

Which words gave you trouble?
Use a different spelling tool.
Try again.

3— Your teacher will read more items from ads.
You are going to spell new words.
This will give you a chance
to try out your spelling tools.

Note 60

Use your spelling tools.

Say, listen, and write.

Make a word family.

Divide and conquer.

Use a spelling rule.

Look for tricky parts.

① Wanted: _____ and _____
② _____ Better _____
③ Looking _____ give-_____
④ _____ to trade _____?
⑤ _____ away _____
⑥ Stereo for sale: Good _____
⑦ Call _____ 6 _____ 11 p.m.
⑧ _____ me _____ you need!

4— Check your spelling.
Your teacher will help you.

Which words gave you trouble?
Use a different spelling tool.
Try again.

Applying your spelling tools

1— Look at this example.

Roy put an ad
on the memo board at work.

He is selling his DVD Player.
Would you buy Roy's
DVD Player?

For Sale
DVD Player

Good shape
10 years old
$75 or Best Offer

Call Roy: 321-4567
Evenings: from 7 to 10 p.m.

2 — Your turn.

Do you want to sell something?
Do you want to buy something?

Write an ad.

A final word

Which words about ***memo board***
would you like to add
to your dictionary?

Practice words

enjoy	year	mix	relax	bosses
mingle	who	where	staff	Christmas
event	win	stay	games	Saturday

Working with spelling tools

Say, listen, and write.

Say each word.
Listen to each sound.
Write the word as you say it.

relax _____	event _____	mix _____
win _____	mixes _____	

If you say these words slowly,
you will have a good chance
of spelling them right.

Make a word family.

Say this word: **mingle**

Think of words that rhyme.
Write the words.
Your teacher will help you with the spelling.

Note 61

mingle _____   _____   _____

_____   _____   _____

Look at your words.
Circle the words that belong
to the same word family as **mingle**.

Learn to spell one of these words, and
you will be able to spell
all of the words.

Say this word: **year**

Think of words that rhyme.
Write the words.
Your teacher will help you with the spelling.

Note 62

year _____   _____   _____

_____   _____   _____

_____   _____   _____

_____   _____   _____

Look at your words.
Circle the words that belong
to the same word family as **year**.

Learn to spell one of these words, and
you will be able to spell
all of the words.

Divide and conquer.

How can you divide and conquer
these words?

enjoy _____

bosses _____

where _____

Christmas _____

Saturday _____

games _____

relax _____

year _____

mixes _____

Divide and conquer

Do you see

❏ **common beginning parts?**

❏ **common end parts?**

❏ **little words?**

Use a spelling rule.

Practice the *Doubling* rule.

Say the base word.
Add the end part to the base word.
Say the new word.

win + ing _____

win + s _____

win + er _____

mix*+ er _____

mix + ed _____

mix + ing _____

mix + s _____

Doubling rule

**If a word has ONE syllable
and ends with ONE vowel
and ONE consonant,
double the final consonant
when you add an end part
that starts with a vowel.**

*Do not use the *Doubling* rule with the letter **x**.
You never see **xx** in English spelling.

Practice the *Silent E* rule.

Say the word.
Underline the long vowel sound.
Circle the silent **e**.

> game

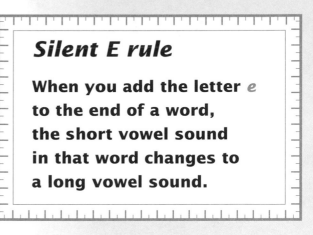

Silent E rule

**When you add the letter *e*
to the end of a word,
the short vowel sound
in that word changes to
a long vowel sound.**

Practice the *Drop the E* rule.

Say the base word.
Add the end part to the base word.
Say the new word.

game   + ing   _____

game   + s   _____

mingle + s   _____

mingle + er   _____

mingle + ing   _____

mingle + ed   _____

Drop the E rule

**If your word ends with
a *silent e*,
drop the *silent e*
before you add an end part
that starts with a vowel.**

Look for tricky parts.

Look at the words below.
Look for the tricky parts.
Use the six steps to help you
spell the words.

who   _____

stay   _____

Saturday   _____

boss   _____

staff   _____

Remember to...

1. **Read the word slowly.**

2. **Mark any tricky part.**

3. **Study the tricky part.**

4. **Cover the word.**

5. **Write the word.**

6. **Check the spelling.**

Trying out your spelling tools

1— Your teacher will read ideas from a poster.
Listen.
Finish the ideas.

Note 63

① It's the _____ _____
   party.
② It's the biggest _____ of the
   _____!
③ Meet the _____.
④ Play _____.
⑤ _____ prizes!
⑥ _____ is it? It's in Block 33.
⑦ When is it? _____.
⑧ _____ can say *no* to this?
⑨ _____! _____ all day!
⑩ _____! _____! _____
   _____!

Use your spelling tools.

Say, listen, and write.

Make a word family.

Divide and conquer.

Use a spelling rule.

Look for tricky parts.

2— Check your spelling.
Your teacher will help you.

Which words gave you trouble?
Use a different spelling tool.
Try again.

3— Your teacher will read another poster.
You are going to spell new words.
This will give you a chance
to try out your spelling tools.

① Are you a good _____?

② Do you like _____ games?

③ Would you like a fun _____ day?

④ _____ sign _____

_____.

⑤ Have no _____!

⑥ _____ _____ on

and take _____.

⑦ When? _____ from 9 a.m. to

noon.

⑧ Who _____? ⑨ You

_____ _____ a big

_____!

Use your spelling tools.

Say, listen, and write.

Make a word family.

Divide and conquer.

Use a spelling rule.

Look for tricky parts.

4— Check your spelling.
Your teacher will help you.

Which words gave you trouble?
Use a different spelling tool.
Try again.

Applying your spelling tools

1— Look at this example.

Here is a poster.
What's it for?
Would you go?

SUMMER RACES

Take part in our
30-km race.

FREE t-shirts!
FREE drinks!

Entry cost: $10

Sign up NOW!

 **2—** Your turn.

Your boss asks you to make a poster.
The poster is for the staff barbecue.

Big Barbecue!

A final word

Which words about **_work relations_**
would you like to add
to your dictionary?

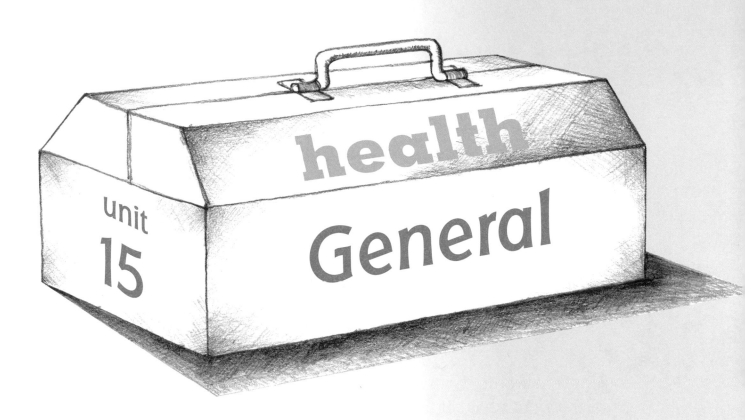

Practice words

hope	back	better	pain	sore
head	hurts	hot	ache	fever
drugs	test	throat	bed	sick

Working with spelling tools

Say, listen, and write.

Say each word.
Listen to each sound.
Write the word as you say it.

fever _____	hot _____	bed _____
drug _____	test _____	

If you say these words slowly,
you will have a good chance
of spelling them right.

Make a word family.

Say this word: **pain**

Think of words that rhyme.
Write the words.
Your teacher will help you with the spelling.

Note 65

pain
_____ _____ _____
_____ _____ _____
_____ _____ _____
_____ _____ _____

Look at your words.
Circle the words that belong
to the same word family as **pain**.

Learn to spell one of these words, and
you will be able to spell all of the words.

Say this word: **throat**

Think of words that rhyme.
Write the words.
Your teacher will help you with the spelling.

Note 66

throat
_____ _____ _____
_____ _____ _____
_____ _____ _____
_____ _____ _____

Look at your words.
Circle the words that belong
to the same word family as **throat**.

Learn to spell one of these words, and
you will be able to spell all of the words.

Say this word: **back**

Think of words that rhyme.
Write the words.
Your teacher will help you with the spelling.

Note
67

back		

Look at your words.
Circle the words that belong to the same word family as **back**.

Learn to spell one of these words, and
you will be able to spell
all of the words.

Say this word: **sick**

Think of words that rhyme.
Write the words.
Your teacher will help you with the spelling.

Note
68

sick		

Look at your words.
Circle the words that belong
to the same word family as **sick**.

Learn to spell one of these words, and
you will be able to spell
all of the words.

Divide and conquer.

How can you divide and conquer these words?

hurts   _____

drugs   _____

Use a spelling rule.

Practice the *Doubling* rule.

Say the base word.
Add the end part to the base word.
Say the new word.

hot   + er   _____

drug   + ed   _____

drug   + s   _____

drug   + ing   _____

bed   + s   _____

bed   + ing   _____

bet   + s   _____

bet   + ing   _____

bet   + er   _____

Bet   + y   _____

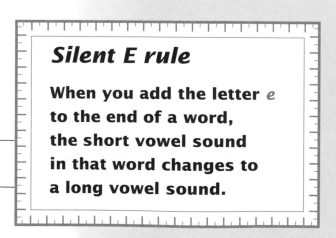

Doubling rule

If a word has ONE syllable and ends with ONE vowel and ONE consonant, double the final consonant when you add an end part that starts with a vowel.

Practice the *Silent E* rule.

Say the word.
Underline the long vowel sound.
Circle the silent **e**.

hope   sore   ache

Silent E rule

When you add the letter *e* to the end of a word, the short vowel sound in that word changes to a long vowel sound.

Practice the *Drop the E* rule.

Say the base word.
Add the end part to the base word.
Say the new word.

hope + ed   _____

hope + ing _____

hope + s   _____

sore + er   _____

sore + s   _____

ache + s   _____

ache + ing _____

ache + ed   _____

ache + y   _____

Drop the E rule

**If your word ends with
a *silent e*,
drop the *silent e*
before you add an end part
that starts with a vowel.**

Look for tricky parts.

Look at the words below.
Look for the tricky parts.
Use the six steps to help you spell the word.

hurt   _____

ache _____

head _____

Remember to...

1. **Read the word slowly.**

2. **Mark any tricky part.**

3. **Study the tricky part.**

4. **Cover the word.**

5. **Write the word.**

6. **Check the spelling.**

· word origins ·

hog-wild

Hogs become wild
when they're excited.
So, someone who is wildly excited
is *hog-wild*.

Trying out your spelling tools

1— Your teacher will read a paragraph.
Listen. Finish the ideas.

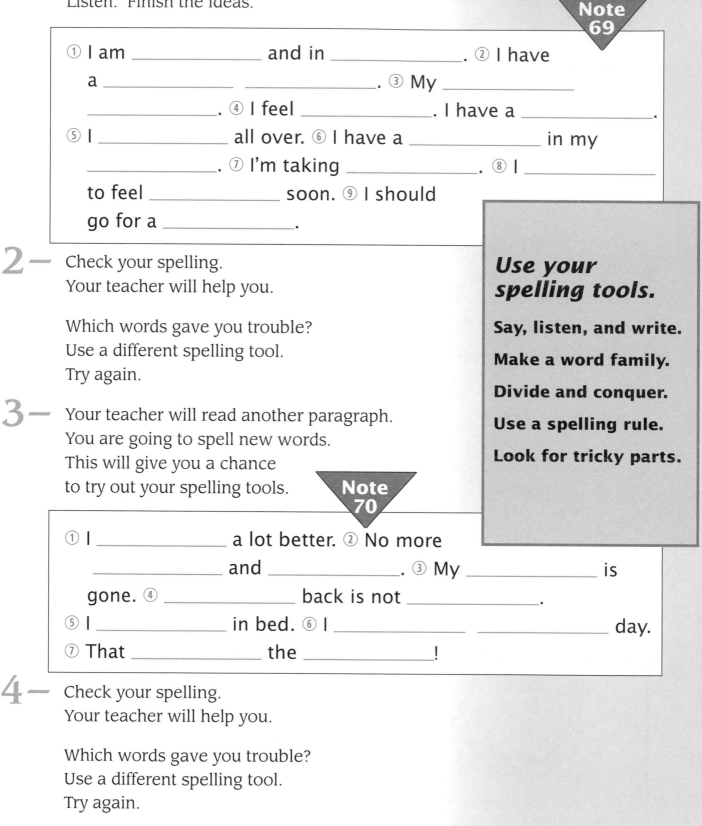

① I am _____ and in _____. ② I have
a _____ _____. ③ My _____
_____. ④ I feel _____. I have a _____.
⑤ I _____ all over. ⑥ I have a _____ in my
_____. ⑦ I'm taking _____. ⑧ I _____
to feel _____ soon. ⑨ I should
go for a _____.

▽ Note 69

2— Check your spelling.
Your teacher will help you.

Which words gave you trouble?
Use a different spelling tool.
Try again.

3— Your teacher will read another paragraph.
You are going to spell new words.
This will give you a chance
to try out your spelling tools.

▽ Note 70

① I _____ a lot better. ② No more
_____ and _____. ③ My _____ is
gone. ④ _____ back is not _____.
⑤ I _____ in bed. ⑥ I _____ _____ day.
⑦ That _____ the _____!

**Use your
spelling tools.**

Say, listen, and write.

Make a word family.

Divide and conquer.

Use a spelling rule.

Look for tricky parts.

4— Check your spelling.
Your teacher will help you.

Which words gave you trouble?
Use a different spelling tool.
Try again.

Applying your spelling tools

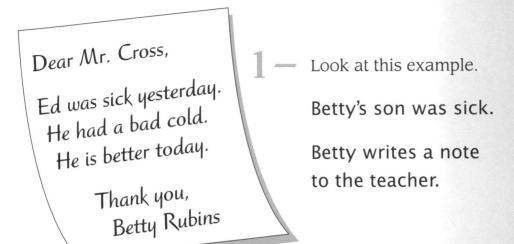

Dear Mr. Cross,

Ed was sick yesterday.
He had a bad cold.
He is better today.

Thank you,
Betty Rubins

1— Look at this example.

Betty's son was sick.

Betty writes a note
to the teacher.

2— Your turn.

Your child
was sick yesterday.
Write a note
to the teacher.

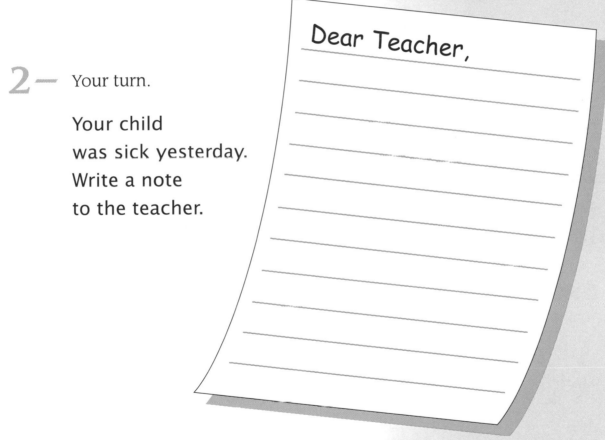

Dear Teacher,

A final word

Which words about **general health**
would you like to add
to your dictionary?

Practice words

diet	cook	gravy	greens	juice
water	sugar	candy	fresh	fats
meat	drink	eat	fish	chicken

Working with spelling tools

Say, listen, and write.

Say each word.
Listen to each sound.
Write the word as you say it.

diet	_____	fat	_____
fresh	_____	fish	_____

If you say these words slowly,
you will have a good chance
of spelling them right.

Make a word family.

Say this word: **drink**

Think of words that rhyme.
Write the words.
Your teacher will help you with the spelling.

Note 71

```
drink _____  _____

_____  _____  _____

_____  _____  _____
```

Look at your words.
Circle the words that belong
to the same word family as **drink**.

Learn to spell one of these words, and
you will be able to spell
all of the words.

Say these words: **eat   meat**

Think of words that rhyme.
Write the words.

Your teacher will help you with the spelling.

Note 72

```
eat  _____  _____
meat _____  _____

_____  _____  _____

_____  _____  _____
```

Look at your words.
Circle the words that belong to the same word family as **eat** and **meat**.

Learn to spell one of these words, and
you will be able to spell
all of the words.

Say this word: **cook**

Think of words that rhyme.

Write the words.

Your teacher will help you with the spelling. ▼ **Note 73**

cook		

Look at your words.

Circle the words that belong to the same word family as **cook**.

Learn to spell one of these words, and
you will be able to spell all of the words.

Divide and conquer.

How can you divide and conquer
these words?

greens	_____
fats	_____
meat	_____
chicken	_____

Divide and conquer

Do you see
- ❑ **common beginning parts?**
- ❑ **common end parts?**
- ❑ **little words?**

Use a spelling rule.

Practice the *Doubling* rule.

Say the base word.
Add the end part to the base word.
Say the new word.

fat + er	_____
fat + s	_____
fat + y	_____

Doubling rule

**If a word has ONE syllable
and ends with ONE vowel
and ONE consonant,
double the final consonant
when you add an end part
that starts with a vowel.**

Practice the *Y* rule (part 1).

Say the word.
Divide the word into two syllables.
Underline the letter that
makes the long **e** sound.

candy   _____

gravy   _____

fatty   _____

Practice the *Y* rule (part 2).

Say the base word.
Add the end part to the base word.
Say the new word.

candy + s   _____

candy + ed   _____

gravy + s   _____

fatty + er   _____

Practice the *Drop the E* rule.

Say the base word.
Add the end part to the base word.
Say the new word.

juice + ed   _____

juice + ing   _____

juice + y   _____

juice + er   _____

juice + s   _____

Y rule (part 1)

**When you hear
the *long e* sound
at the end of a word
that has two syllables,
use *y*.**

**You have a good chance
of being right.**

Y rule (part 2)

**If a word ends in
consonant + y,
the *y* changes to *i*
when you add all end parts
except *ing*.**

Drop the E rule

**If your word ends with
a *silent e*,
drop the *silent e*
before you add an end part
that starts with a vowel.**

Look for tricky parts.

Look at the words below.
Look for the tricky parts.
Use the six steps to help you spell the word.

green _____

sugar _____

juice _____

water _____

chicken _____

Remember to...

1. Read the word slowly.
2. Mark any tricky part.
3. Study the tricky part.
4. Cover the word.
5. Write the word.
6. Check the spelling.

Trying out your spelling tools

1— Your teacher will read some ideas about diet.
Listen.
Finish the ideas.

Note 74

① _____ _____ _____.

② Cut down on red _____.

③ _____ more _____ and _____.

④ _____ _____ and fruit _____.

⑤ Say no to _____, _____ and _____.

⑥ Don't buy _____.

⑦ Watch your _____. Live to be a hundred!

Use your spelling tools.

Say, listen, and write.

Make a word family.

Divide and conquer.

Use a spelling rule.

Look for tricky parts.

2— Check your spelling.
Your teacher will help you.

Which words gave you trouble?
Use a different spelling tool.
Try again.

3— Your teacher will read a passage.

You are going to spell new words.
This will give you a chance to try out your spelling tools.

Note 75

① My dad _____ meat every day. ② He _____ _____ food. ③ He _____ all the time.

④ He _____ _____ _____ great.

⑤ He never eats _____.

⑥ My dad is 99 _____ old.

⑦ _____ did he _____ to be so old? ⑧ _____ _____ stuff is _____.

Use your spelling tools.

Say, listen, and write.

Make a word family.

Divide and conquer.

Use a spelling rule.

Look for tricky parts.

4— Check your spelling.
Your teacher will help you.

Which words gave you trouble?
Use a different spelling tool.
Try again.

Applying your spelling tools

1— Look at this example.

Hank thinks about his diet.

Here are the good things
about his diet—
and the bad things, too!

Good things:
1. I drink lots of water.
2. I like popcorn.

Bad things:
1. I eat a lot of fast food.
2. I drink too much coffee.

I should
- cook food at home
- cut down on coffee

Think about your diet.
Write down some good things
and bad things.

Good things: _Apples_
bnanas milk tofu

Bad things: _Candy_

I should

A final word

Which words about **diet**
would you like to add
to your dictionary?

Practice words

run	jog	hike	trim	mind
workout	body	self	sleep	tired
smoke	keep	fit	kinds	stress

Working with spelling tools

Say, listen, and write.

Say each word.
Listen to each sound.
Write the word as you say it.

run _____	trim _____	jog _____
fit _____	mind _____	self _____
kind _____		

If you say these words slowly,
you will have a good chance of spelling them right.

Make a word family.

Say this word: **out**

Think of words that rhyme.
Write the words.
Your teacher will help you with the spelling.

Note 76

out _____ _____
_____ _____ _____
_____ _____ _____

Look at your words.
Circle the words that belong to the same word family as **out**.

Learn to spell one of these words, and
you will be able to spell
all of the words.

Say these words: **keep**   **sleep**

Think of words that rhyme.
Write the words.

Your teacher will help you with the spelling.

Note 77

keep _____ _____
sleep _____ _____
_____ _____ _____
_____ _____ _____

Look at your words.
Circle the words that belong to the same word family as **keep** and **sleep**.

Learn to spell one of these words, and
you will be able to spell
all of the words.

Say this word: **stress**

Think of words that rhyme.
Write the words.
Your teacher will help you with the spelling.

Note
78

stress _____ _____

_____ _____ _____

_____ _____ _____

Look at your words.
Circle the words that belong to the same word family as **stress**.

Learn to spell one of these words, and
you will be able to spell all of the words.

Divide and conquer.

How can you divide and conquer
these words?

kinds	_____
workout	_____

Divide and conquer

Do you see
☐ **common beginning parts?**
☐ **common end parts?**
☐ **little words?**

Use a spelling rule.

Practice the _Doubling_ rule.

Say the base word.
Add the end part to the base word.
Say the new word.

run	+ ing	_____
run	+ s	_____
run	+ er	_____
run	+ y	_____

Doubling rule

**If a word has ONE syllable
and ends with ONE vowel
and ONE consonant,
double the final consonant
when you add an end part
that starts with a vowel.**

```
trim + s     _____
trim + er    _____
trim + ing   _____
trim + ed    _____
fit  + ed    _____
fit  + ing   _____
fit  + s     _____
jog  + s     _____
jog  + ed    _____
jog  + er    _____
jog  + ing   _____
```

Doubling rule

If a word has ONE syllable and ends with ONE vowel and ONE consonant, double the final consonant when you add an end part that starts with a vowel.

Practice the Y rule (part 1).

Say the word.
Divide the word into two syllables.
Underline the letter that
makes the long **e** sound.

```
body    _____
runny   _____
```

Y rule (part 1)

**When you hear
the *long e* sound
at the end of a word
that has two syllables,
use *y*.**

**You have a good chance
of being right.**

Y rule (part 2)

**If a word ends in
consonant + y,
the *y* changes to *i*
when you add all end parts
except *ing*.**

Practice the Y rule (part 2).

Say the base word.
Add the end part to the base word.
Say the new word

```
body  + s    _____
runny + er   _____
```

Practice the *Silent E* rule.

Say the word.
Underline the
long vowel sound.
Circle the silent **e**.

tire	smoke	hike

> ## Silent E rule
>
> **When you add the letter *e*
> to the end of a word,
> the short vowel sound in that word
> changes to a long vowel sound.**

Practice the *Drop the E* rule.

Say the base word.
Add the end part to the base word.
Say the new word.

tire + ed   _____

tire + ing   _____

tire + s   _____

smoke + er   _____

smoke + ing   _____

smoke + ed   _____

smoke + s   _____

smoke + y   _____

hike + ing   _____

hike + s   _____

hike + er   _____

hike + ed   _____

> ## Drop the E rule
>
> **If your word ends with
> a *silent e*,
> drop the *silent e*
> before you add an end part
> that starts with a vowel.**

Look for tricky parts.

Look at the word below.
Look for the tricky part.
Use the six steps to help you spell the word.

> ## Remember to
>
> 1. Read the word slowly.
> 2. Mark any tricky part.
> 3. Study the tricky part.
> 4. Cover the word.
> 5. Write the word.
> 6. Check the spelling.

work	_____

Trying out your spelling tools

1— Your teacher will read some information.
Listen. Finish the ideas.

Note 79

① How to stay _____ and _____.

② Your _____ needs care. ③ _____ when you are _____. ④ Do all _____ of exercise. ⑤ Go for a _____. ⑥ _____, _____ or _____. ⑦ Cut down on _____. ⑧ Don't _____. ⑨ _____ and _____ fit.

2— Check your spelling.
Your teacher will help you.

Which words gave you trouble?
Use a different spelling tool. Try again.

3— Your teacher will read more information.
You are going to spell new words.
This will give you a chance
to try out your spelling tools.

Note 80

Use your spelling tools.

Say, listen, and write.

Make a word family.

Divide and conquer.

Use a spelling rule.

Look for tricky parts.

① _____ fit.
② What _____ this mean? ③ It means more than _____. ④ It means _____ than _____. ⑤ It means more _____ not _____. ⑥ Keeping fit means thinking _____ _____ needs. ⑦ It means being _____ to _____.

4— Check your spelling.
Your teacher will help you.

Which words gave you trouble?
Use a different spelling tool. Try again.

Applying your spelling tools

1. How often do you exercise?
○ never ✖ sometimes ○ always

2. What do you do for exercise?
○ bike ○ jog ✖ walk
○ swim ○ other

3. When do you exercise?
○ mornings ○ afternoons
✖ at night ○ weekends

4. Are you in good shape?
○ very good ○ good
✖ so-so ○ not good

1— Look at this example.

Lana goes to the clinic.
She fills out a form.

Is Lana fit?

2— Your turn.

You get this in the mail.

Fill it out
and get a free visit
to Gym Land.

ONE TIME OFFER

One free visit to Gym Land
Just fill this form.

Do you like to exercise?
_____

What do you do for exercise?
_____

When do you exercise?
_____

Are you fit?

_____

See you at the gym!

A final word

Which words about *fitness*
would you like to add
to your dictionary?

Practice words

life	change	partner	expect	felt
recover	sad	lonely	tempted	cope
could	again	stunned	rethink	discover

Working with spelling tools

Say, listen, and write.

Say each word.
Listen to each sound.
Write the word as you say it.

expect _____	sad _____	felt _____
rethink _____	partner _____	tempted _____

If you say these words slowly,
you will have a good chance
of spelling them right.

Make a word family.

Say this word: **could**

Think of words that rhyme.
Write the words.
Your teacher will help you with the spelling.

Note
81

 could _____ _____

_____ _____ _____

_____ _____

Look at your words.
Circle the words that belong
to the same word family as **could**.

Learn to spell one of these words, and
you will be able to spell
all of the words.

Divide and conquer.

How can you divide and conquer
these words?

partner _____
lonely _____
tempted _____
again _____
discover _____
rethink _____
recover _____

Divide and conquer

Do you see
☐ **common beginning parts?**
☐ **common end parts?**
☐ **little words?**

Use a spelling rule.

Practice the *Doubling* rule.

Say the base word.
Add the end part to the base word.
Say the new word.

sad + er	_____
stun + s	_____
stun + ing	_____
stun + ed	_____
stun + er	_____

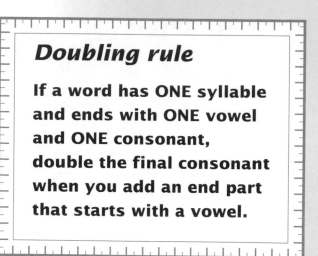

Doubling rule

If a word has ONE syllable and ends with ONE vowel and ONE consonant, double the final consonant when you add an end part that starts with a vowel.

Practice the *Silent E* rule.

Say the word.
Underline the long vowel sound.
Circle the silent **e**.

life	cope	change	lone

Silent E rule

When you add the letter *e* to the end of a word, the short vowel sound in that word changes to a long vowel sound.

Practice the *Drop the E* rule.

Say the base word.
Add the end part to the base word.
Say the new word.

life + er	_____
lone + er	_____
cope + ing	_____
cope + s	_____
cope + ed	_____
change + ing	_____
change + ed	_____
change + s	_____

Drop the E rule

If your word ends with a *silent e*, drop the *silent e* before you add an end part that starts with a vowel.

Look for the tricky parts.

Look at the words below.
Look for the tricky parts.
Use the six steps to help you spell the word.

again	_____
cover	_____

Remember to . . .

1. **Read the word slowly.**

2. **Mark any tricky part.**

3. **Study the tricky part.**

4. **Cover the word.**

5. **Write the word.**

6. **Check the spelling.**

Trying out your spelling tools

1 — Your teacher will read the first part of a short story.
Listen.
Finish the ideas.

Note 82

① Did my _____ ever _____!
② My _____ left me. ③ I did not
_____ it. ④ I _____
_____. ⑤ I was _____ and
_____. ⑥ I was _____ to
give up.

⑦ What _____ I do? ⑧ I had to
_____ and _____. ⑨ I had to
start _____. ⑩ I started to
_____ my life. ⑪ I started to
_____ a new life.

Use your spelling tools.

Say, listen, and write.

Make a word family.

Divide and conquer.

Use a spelling rule.

Look for tricky parts.

2 — Check your spelling.
Your teacher will help you.

Which words gave you troublc?
Use a different spelling tool.
Try again.

3— Your teacher will read the rest of the short story.
You are going to spell new words.
This will give you a chance
to try out your spelling tools.

Note 83

① I was _____. ② I started

_____ in the mornings.

③ _____ people were walking, too.

④ _____ a few _____, we

were friends. ⑤ They _____ my

_____ of the dawn.

⑥ There was _____. ⑦ I _____

survive the break-up!

Use your spelling tools.

Say, listen, and write.

Make a word family.

Divide and conquer.

Use a spelling rule.

Look for tricky parts.

4— Check your spelling.
Your teacher will help you.

Which words gave you trouble?
Use a different spelling tool.
Try again.

Applying your spelling tools

1— Look at this example
of a journal entry.

Terry's dog passed away.
How does Terry feel?

March 21

I still feel sad about Micky.
I loved that silly dog.
They say I should get a puppy.
They say it would be good for my mental health.
Maybe in a few months.

2 — Your turn.

Think about a change in your life.
Did the change make you feel
happy or sad?

Make a journal entry.

A final word

Which words about **changes**
would you like to add to your dictionary?

unit 19

writings

Lists

Practice words

send	stamps	call	up	fax
feed	wash	return	mail	bank
gift	present	wedding	remind	go

Working with spelling tools

Say, listen, and write.

Say each word.
Listen to each sound.
Write the word as you say it.

send _____	up _____	stamp _____
gift _____	go _____	fax _____

If you say these words slowly,
you will have a good chance
of spelling them right.

Make a word family.

Say this word: **call**

Think of words that rhyme.
Write the words.

Your teacher will help you with the spelling.

Note 84

call

Look at your words.
Circle the words that belong to the same word family as **call**.

Learn to spell one of these words, and
you will be able to spell all of the words.

Say this word: **feed**

Think of words that rhyme.
Write the words.

Your teacher will help you with the spelling.

Note 85

feed

Look at your words.
Circle the words that belong to the same word family as **feed**.

Learn to spell one of these words, and
you will be able to spell all of the words.

Say this word: **bank**

Think of words that rhyme.
Write the words.

Your teacher will help you with the spelling.

Note
86

bank _____ _____

_____ _____ _____

_____ _____ _____

Look at your words.
Circle the words that belong to the same word family as **bank**.

Learn to spell one of these words, and
you will be able to spell
all of the words.

Say this word: **mail**

Think of words that rhyme.
Write the words.

Your teacher will help you with the spelling.

Note
87

mail _____ _____

_____ _____ _____

_____ _____ _____

_____ _____ _____

Look at your words.
Circle the words that belong to the same word family as **mail**.

Learn to spell one of these words, and
you will be able to spell
all of the words.

Divide and conquer.

How can you divide and conquer these words?

stamps _____

return _____

remind _____

present _____

Use a spelling rule.

Practice the *Doubling* rule.

Say the base word.
Add the end part to the base word.
Say the new word.

wed + ing _____

fax + ed _____

fax + s _____

fax + ing _____

up + er _____

Look for tricky parts.

Look at the words below.
Look for the tricky parts.

Use the six steps
to help you spell the word.

turn _____

wash _____

Trying out your spelling tools

1— Your teacher will read a to-do list.
Listen.
Finish the list.

Note 88

① _____ to _____
② _____ fish — _____ vet
③ _____ videos
④ _____ _____ — buy
_____
⑤ _____ out socks
⑥ _____ _____ to Max
⑦ _____ Hank to pick _____
_____

> ### Use your spelling tools.
>
> **Say, listen, and write.**
>
> **Make a word family.**
>
> **Divide and conquer.**
>
> **Use a spelling rule.**
>
> **Look for tricky parts.**

2— Check your spelling.
Your teacher will help you.

Which words gave you trouble?
Use a different spelling tool. Try again.

3— Your teacher will read another to-do list.
You are going to spell new words.
This will give you a chance
to try out your spelling tools.

Note 89

① _____ _____ stamps
② stop _____ _____ —
_____
③ buy _____ for pictures
④ send _____ _____ card
⑤ _____ : _____ change today
⑥ _____ _____
_____ before _____
to work ⑦ _____ after a hard day

> ### Use your spelling tools.
>
> **Say, listen, and write.**
>
> **Make a word family.**
>
> **Divide and conquer.**
>
> **Use a spelling rule.**
>
> **Look for tricky parts.**

4— Check your spelling.
Your teacher will help you.

Which words gave you trouble?
Use a different spelling tool.
Try again.

Applying your spelling tools

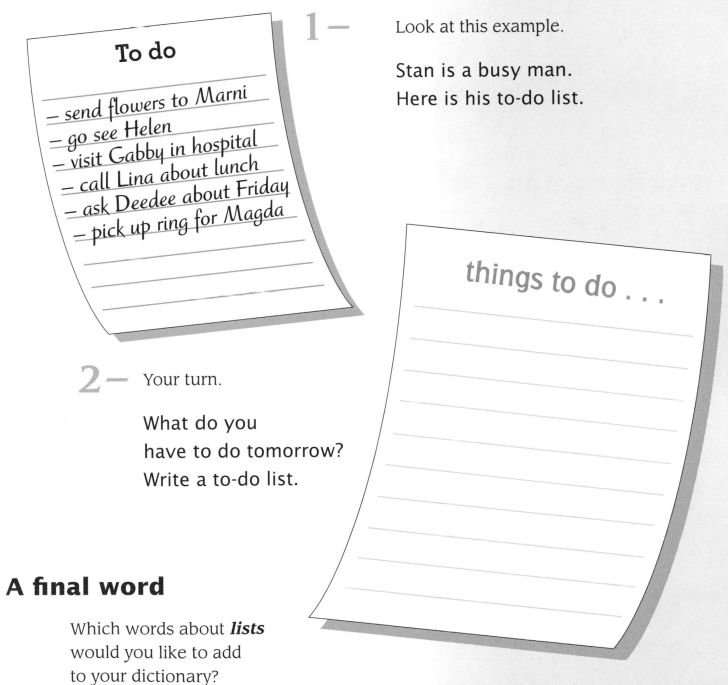

To do

— send flowers to Marni
— go see Helen
— visit Gabby in hospital
— call Lina about lunch
— ask Deedee about Friday
— pick up ring for Magda

1— Look at this example.

Stan is a busy man.
Here is his to-do list.

2— Your turn.

What do you
have to do tomorrow?
Write a to-do list.

things to do . . .

A final word

Which words about **lists**
would you like to add
to your dictionary?

unit 20

writings

Dear Diary

Practice words

wow	very	ignore	today	went
seemed	everyone	dear	said	saw
says	nothing	there	tomorrow	same

Working with spelling tools

Say, listen, and write.

Say the word.
Listen to each sound.
Write the word as you say it.

went _____

If you say this word slowly,
you will have a good chance
of spelling it right.

Make a word family.

Say this word: **wow**

Think of words that rhyme.
Write the words.
Your teacher will help you with the spelling.

Note
90

wow

Look at your words.
Circle the words that belong
to the same word family as **wow**.

Learn to spell one of these words, and
you will be able to spell
all of the words.

Say this word: **dear**

Think of words that rhyme.
Write the words.

Your teacher will help you with the spelling.

Note
91

dear

Look at your words.
Circle the words that belong to the same word family as **dear**.

Learn to spell one of these words, and
you will be able to spell
all of the words.

Say this word: **saw**

Think of words that rhyme.
Write the words.

Your teacher will help you with the spelling.

Note 92

_____ saw _____   _____   _____

_____   _____   _____

_____   _____   _____

_____   _____   _____

Look at your words.
Circle the words that belong to
the same word family as **saw**.

Learn to spell one of these words, and
you will be able to spell
all of the words.

Divide and conquer.

How can you divide and conquer
these words?

today   _____

everyone   _____

there   _____

dear   _____

says   _____

tomorrow   _____

seemed   _____

nothing   _____

Divide and conquer

Do you see
❑ **common beginning parts?**
❑ **common end parts?**
❑ **little words?**

Use a spelling rule.

Practice the *Y* rule (part 1).

Say the word.
Divide the word into two syllables.
Underline the letter that
makes the long **e** sound.

very	_____

Practice the *Silent E* rule.

Say the word.
Underline the long vowel sound.
Circle the silent **e**.

same	_____
ignore	_____

Practice the *Drop the E* rule.

Say the base word.
Add the end part to the base word.
Say the new word.

ignore + ed	_____
ignore + ing	_____
ignore + s	_____

Look for tricky parts.

Look at the words below.
Look for the tricky parts.
Use the six steps to help you
spell the words.

very _____
everyone _____
seem _____
said _____
tomorrow _____

Remember to...

1. **Read the word slowly.**
2. **Mark any tricky part.**
3. **Study the tricky part.**
4. **Cover the word.**
5. **Write the word.**
6. **Check the spelling.**

Trying out your spelling tools

1— Your teacher will read a diary entry.
Listen.
Finish the ideas.

Note 93

① _____ *Diary,*
② _____! ③ _____ *was*
_____ *strange.* ④ *I* _____ *to*
work. ⑤ _____ _____
seemed weird. ⑥ *They* _____ *to*
_____ *me.* ⑦ *I* _____ *Bonny.*
⑧ *I* _____, *"What's up?"* ⑨ *Bonny*
_____, *"Oh,* _____.*"*
⑩ *I hope* _____ *isn't the*
_____.

Use your spelling tools.

Say, listen, and write.

Make a word family.

Divide and conquer.

Use a spelling rule.

Look for tricky parts.

2— Check your spelling.
Your teacher will help you.

Which words gave you trouble?
Use a different spelling tool. Try again.

3— Your teacher will read another diary entry. You are going to spell new words. This will give you a chance to try out your spelling tools.

Note 94

Note 94

Use your spelling tools.

Say, listen, and write.

Make a word family.

Divide and conquer.

Use a spelling rule.

Look for tricky parts.

Dear Diary,
① *Things are not as bad* _____ *they* _____ . ② *I* _____ _____ *work today.* ③ *Everyone starts* _____ *"Happy Birthday."*
④ _____ *had a cake* _____ . ⑤ *I* _____ *never forget* _____ *I felt.*

4— Check your spelling. Your teacher will help you.

Which words gave you trouble? Use a different spelling tool. Try again.

Applying your spelling tools

1— Look at this example.

Here is what Cory wrote in his diary.

What kind of day did he have?

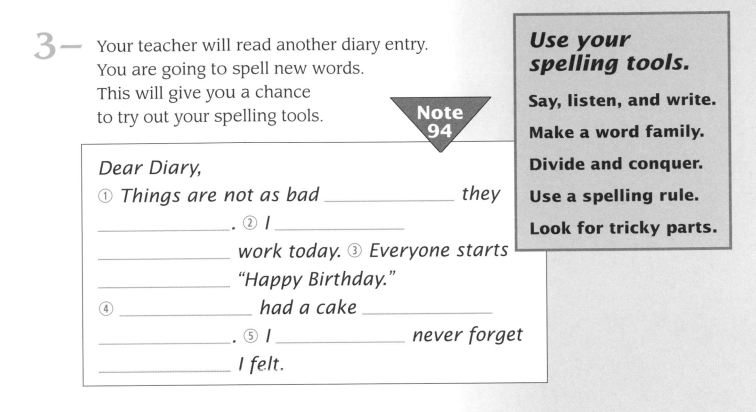

Dear Diary,
I found $25.
My boss
gave me
the day off.
I met a real
nice woman!

What a lucky day! I feel good just writing about it.

2 — Your turn.

Think of three things
that happened to you today.

Write them down in your diary.

A final word

Which words about **Dear Diary**
would you like to add
to your dictionary?

Practice words

howdy	card	say	way	hear
done	well	must	excited	proud
let	goes	sorry	good	pretty

Working with spelling tools

Say, listen, and write.

Say each word.
Listen to each sound.
Write the word as you say it.

card _____   must _____   let _____

If you say these words slowly,
you will have a good chance
of spelling them right.

Make a word family.

Say these words: **way**   **say**

Think of words that rhyme.
Write the words.
Your teacher will help you with the spelling.

Note 95

way		
say		

Look at your words.
Circle the words that belong
to the same word family as **say** and **way**.

Learn to spell one of these words, and
you will be able to spell
all of the words.

Say this word: **well**

Think of words that rhyme.
Write the words.

Your teacher will help you with the spelling.

Note 96

well		

Look at your words.
Circle the words that belong to the same word family as **well**.

Learn to spell one of these words, and
you will be able to spell
all of the words.

Divide and conquer.

How can you divide and conquer these words?

Divide and conquer

Do you see
- ☐ common beginning parts?
- ☐ common end parts?
- ☐ little words?

howdy _____

hear _____

goes _____

Use a spelling rule.

Practice the *Doubling* rule.

Say the base word.
Add the end part to the base word.
Say the new word.

let + ing _____

let + s _____

let + er _____

Let + y _____

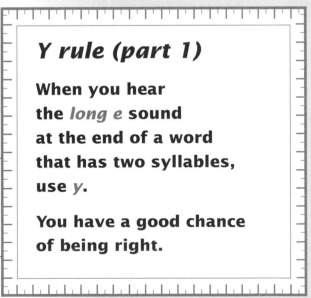

Doubling rule

If a word has ONE syllable and ends with ONE vowel and ONE consonant, double the final consonant when you add an end part that starts with a vowel.

Practice the *Y* rule (part 1).

Say the word.
Divide the word into two syllables.
Underline the letter that
makes the long **e** sound.

howdy _____

sorry _____

pretty _____

Y rule (part 1)

**When you hear
the *long e* sound
at the end of a word
that has two syllables,
use *y*.**

**You have a good chance
of being right.**

Practice the *Y* rule (part 2).

Say the base word.
Add the end part to the base word.
Say the new word.

sorry + er _____
pretty + er _____

Y rule (part 2)

If a word ends in
consonant + y,
the *y* changes to *i*
when you add all end parts
except *ing*.

Practice the *Silent E* rule.

Say the word.
Underline the long vowel sound.
Circle the silent **e**.

excite

Silent E rule

When you add the letter *e*
to the end of a word,
the short vowel sound
in that word changes to
a long vowel sound.

Practice the *Drop the E* rule.

Say the base word.
Add the end part to the base word.
Say the new word.

excite + ed   _____
excite + ing _____
excite + s   _____

Drop the E rule

If your word ends with
a *silent e*,
drop the *silent e*
before you add an end part
that starts with a vowel.

Look for tricky parts.

Look at the words below.
Look for the tricky parts.
Use the six steps to help you spell the word.

proud _____

sorry _____

good _____

done _____

goes _____

pretty _____

Remember to...

1. **Read the word slowly.**
2. **Mark any tricky part.**
3. **Study the tricky part.**
4. **Cover the word.**
5. **Write the word.**
6. **Check the spelling.**

Trying out your spelling tools

1— Your teacher will read a note.
Listen. Finish the note.

① _____ there, Letty!

② *Just a* _____ *to* _____
*"*_____ _____.*"*

③ *We* _____ *you got a new job.*

④ _____ *to go!* _____ *work!*

⑤ *You* _____ *be so* _____.

⑥ *We are so* _____ *of you.* ⑦ *But,*
_____ *to see you go.* ⑧ _____
us know how the job _____.

Tony and the boys

Note 97

Use your spelling tools.

Say, listen, and write.

Make a word family.

Divide and conquer.

Use a spelling rule.

Look for tricky parts.

2— Check your spelling.
Your teacher will help you.

Which words gave you trouble?
Use a different spelling tool. Try again.

3— Your teacher will read a postcard.

You are going to spell new words.
This will give you a chance
to try out your spelling tools.

Note
98

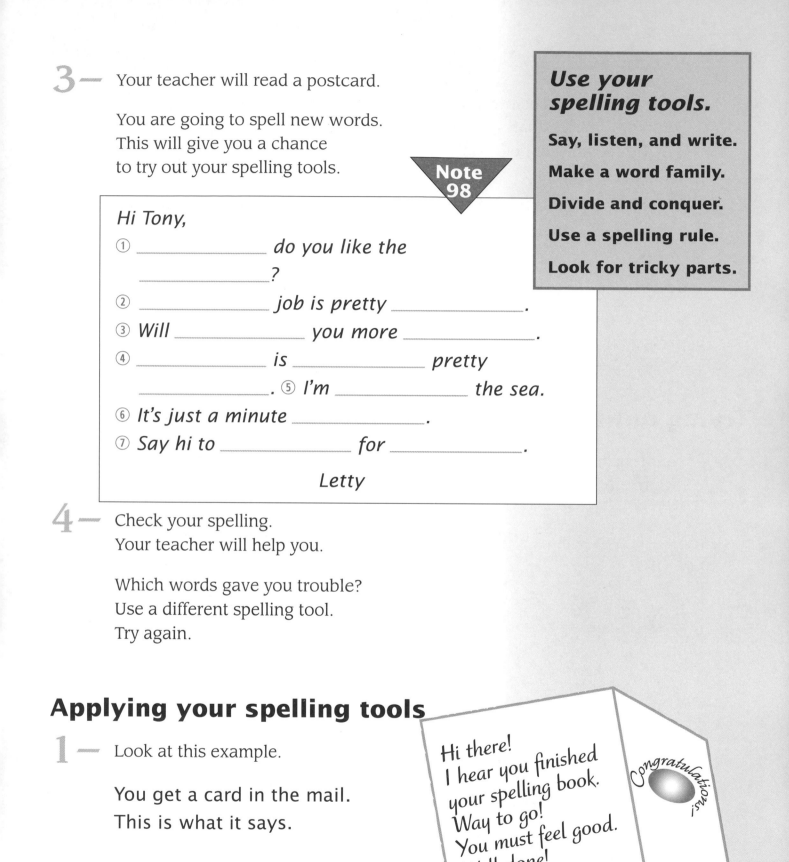

Use your
spelling tools.

Say, listen, and write.

Make a word family.

Divide and conquer.

Use a spelling rule.

Look for tricky parts.

Hi Tony,
① _____ do you like the
_____ ?
② _____ job is pretty _____ .
③ Will _____ you more _____ .
④ _____ is _____ pretty
_____ . ⑤ I'm _____ the sea.
⑥ It's just a minute _____ .
⑦ Say hi to _____ for _____ .
Letty

4— Check your spelling.
Your teacher will help you.

Which words gave you trouble?
Use a different spelling tool.
Try again.

Applying your spelling tools

1— Look at this example.

You get a card in the mail.
This is what it says.

Hi there!
I hear you finished
your spelling book.
Way to go!
You must feel good.
Well done!
A friend.

Congratulations!

2– Your turn.

Answer the note
from your friend.

> Hi there, friend,
>
> I do feel good about finishing my spelling book, thank you for the letter.
>
> from: Josh

A final word

Which words about **notes**
would you like to add
to your dictionary?

The Spelling Toolbox ■ **Workbook 1**

Student Glossary

base word

A base word is a word that has no beginning parts or end parts.

Hat, **jump**, and **sun** are base words.

Hats, **jumped**, and **sunny** are not base words.

consonant

These letters are called consonants:

B C D F G H J K L M
N P Q R S T V W X Z

Sometimes **Y** is a consonant, too.

long vowel sounds

Long vowel sounds say their name.

The following words have long vowel sounds:

make **Pete** **bike** **smoke** **cute**

short vowel sounds

The following words have short vowel sounds:

tap **pet** **sit** **pot** **hut**

syllable

A syllable is a small part of a word.

Most of the time, a syllable has one vowel sound.

The following words all have two syllables:

Fri day **bu sy** **say ing**

vowel

The following letters are called vowels:

A E I O U

Sometimes, the letter **Y** is a vowel, too.

Word List

ache (15)
again (18)
always (12)
April (11)
apt. (11)
away (13)
baby (3)
back (15)
bag (4)
bank (19)
baseball (7)
bed (15)
best (13)
better (15)
bikes (7)
birthday (3)
block (9)
body (17)
bosses (14)
bowling (7)
box (4)
boxes (6)
bread (4)
break (12)
buddy (9)
build (10)
bunch (4)
bus (7)
busy (8)
buy (13)
call (19)
can (5)
candy (16)
card (21)
cards (2)

care (9)
carry (6)
carton (4)
change (18)
chat (2)
cheap (13)
check (5)
chicken (16)
Christmas (14)
church (9)
city (8)
classes (7)
clean (5)
clear (10)
clog (5)
club (9)
coffee(4)
come (3)
cook (16)
cop (9)
cope (18)
could (18)
cry (6)
day (12)
dear (20)
diet (16)
discover (18)
donate (8)
done (21)
door (8)
draft (5)
drink (16)
drive (8)
drugs (15)
DVD (2)

eat (16)
eggs (4)
empty (10)
enjoy (14)
event (14)
everyone (20)
excited (21)
expect (18)
faces (12)
fats (16)
fax (19)
feed (19)
felt (18)
fever (15)
few (4)
finish (11)
fish (16)
fishing (7)
fit (17)
fix (5)
food (8)
found (13)
free (13)
fresh (16)
friends(2)
fruit (4)
fun (3)
games (14)
gas (6)
gift (19)
girl (3)
give (13)
go (19)
goes (21)
good (21)

gravy (16)
greens (16)
hall (8)
happy (3)
head (15)
hear (21)
heat (6)
help (8)
here (3)
hi (9)
hike (17)
hope (15)
hot (15)
hotdogs (4)
howdy (21)
hurts (15)
ignore (20)
jam (4)
Jan. (11)
job (11)
jog (17)
joke (12)
juice (16)
keep (17)
kick (7)
kinds (17)
know (9)
laugh (12)
leaky (5)
learn (11)
let (21)
life (18)
lights (10)
like (11)
lonely (18)

look (6)	phone (8)	send (19)	there (20)
lost (13)	plan (8)	shampoo (4)	things (11)
lots (10)	plant (10)	shape (13)	throat (15)
love (3)	play (12)	shift (12)	time (3)
lug (6)	please (5)	shops (7)	tired (17)
lunch (12)	plug (5)	show (7)	today (20)
made (3)	popcorn (2)	shrubs (10)	together (3)
mail (19)	present (19)	shut (10)	tomorrow (20)
March (11)	pretty (21)	sick (15)	town (7)
meat (16)	prices (10)	sign (12)	toy (13)
meet (8)	proud (21)	skate (7)	trim (17)
milk (4)	put (10)	skills (11)	try (11)
mind (17)	rally (8)	sleep (17)	up (19)
mingle (14)	Rd. (11)	smoke (17)	used (13)
mix (14)	reach (9)	snack (12)	very (20)
month (6)	recover (18)	some (4)	visit (2)
morning (12)	relax (14)	sore (15)	vote (8)
move (6)	remind (19)	sorry (21)	walk (2)
must (21)	remove (5)	soup (12)	wanted (13)
need (8)	rent (6)	sports (7)	wash (19)
never (12)	replace (5)	St. (11)	water (16)
new (10)	rest (2)	staff (14)	way (21)
nice (9)	rethink (18)	stamps (19)	wedding (19)
noon (12)	return (19)	start (11)	weekend (2)
note (3)	ride (13)	stay (14)	well (21)
nothing (20)	rip (5)	street (10)	went (20)
notice (6)	roads (10)	stress (17)	where (14)
offer (13)	run (17)	stunned (18)	who (14)
old (5)	sad (18)	sugar (16)	wider (10)
one (6)	said (20)	summer (7)	win (14)
pack (6)	sale (8)	sun (2)	winter (7)
package (4)	same (20)	Sunday (2)	wish (3)
pain (15)	Saturday (14)	swimming (7)	work (11)
paint (5)	saw (20)	TV (2)	workout (17)
pals (9)	say (21)	take (9)	wow (20)
park (2)	says (20)	talk (2)	year (14)
partner (18)	school (9)	tea (2)	you (6)
party (3)	see (3)	teach (9)	
pave (10)	seemed (20)	tempted (18)	
pay (5)	self (17)	test (15)	
people (9)	sell (13)	thank (6)	

Notes for Users

unit 1 • introduction • Spelling Tools

 Possible responses: bow, low, mow, row, tow, crow, flow, glow, grow, know, slow, snow, stow / go, ho, no, so, pro / dough, though, although / doe, foe, hoe, Joe, toe, / sew / oh

Explain to the student that it is possible to have different spellings for the same sound; therefore, it's a good idea to learn words as groups or families, according to spelling.

Spelling Rules

Doubling rule
If a word is one syllable and ends with one vowel and one consonant, double the final consonant when you add an end part that starts with a vowel.

Y rule
If a word has more than one syllable and ends with the long *e* sound, try using *y* for the long *e* sound.

If a word ends in consonant + *y*, the *y* changes to *i* when adding all suffixes, except *ing*. (If a word ends in vowel + *y*, there is no change when adding suffixes.)

Silent E rule
The short vowel sound becomes a long vowel sound in a CVC (consonant-vowel-consonant) word when *e* is added to the end of the word.

Drop the E rule
If a word ends in silent *e*, drop the *e* when adding a suffix that starts with a vowel. (Keep the *e* when adding a suffix that starts with a consonant.)

 Tricky Part
"Mark the tricky part" means highlight the part in some way (e.g., circling, underlining, highlighting with a marker, separating it off, etc.).

"Study the tricky part" can mean visualizing the part in some way, spelling it out loud, exaggerating the pronunciation, talking about how to remember it, etc.

 Tricky Part
play – You need two letters to make the long *a* sound.
have – The *e* is silent.
roll – There are two *l*'s.
busy – The vowel *u* sounds like the short vowel *i*.

unit 2 • home • Leisure

Possible responses: balk, chalk, stalk / cock, dock, hock, jock, lock, mock, rock, sock, tock, block, clock, crock, flock, frock, knock, smock, Spock, stock / gawk, hawk / doc, wok

Dictation

Suggestion: Read the dictations once through. Then read them again line by line, giving the learner time to fill in the blanks.

1. I (walk) every (Sunday).
2. I like to (visit) my (friends).
3. We (chat) over (tea) or play (cards).
4. We don't like (TV), but we like (DVDs).
5. We make a big bowl of (popcorn) and (talk).
6. Sometimes, we go to the (park) and hang out in the (sun).
7. I love the (weekend). It's my time to (rest).

7 **Dictation**

1. The (best) day of (the) week is (Monday).
2. My (friend) (visits) me (if) she can.
3. It's (dark) by the time she goes home.
4. She's always (running) for the (bus).
5. She's so (funny).
6. My life would seem (humdrum) without her.

unit 3 • **home** • Family Times

8 **Possible responses:** bee, fee, gee, Lee, pee, wee, Cree, free, knee, tree, three, whee / be, he, me, we, she / pea, sea, tea, flea / key

9 **Dictation**

1. Just a (note) to say we have a (baby) (girl).
2. (Happy) you could (come) to the (party).
3. Have a (fun) (birthday). (Love), sis.
4. You (made) our day!
5. (See) you next (time).
6. Let's get (together).
7. (Wish) you were (here).

10 **Dictation**

1. (Hugs) and best (wishes).
2. All of (us) wish (her) the best.
3. Sorry. (We) can't make it.
4. This is (not) a (day) to be missed!
5. Thanks for all the great (times).
6. (Just) want to (say) "Hi."
7. Thanks for the (gift).
8. Do I sound (wishy)-(washy)?

unit 4 • **home** • Shopping

11 **Possible responses:** dead, head, lead, read, tread, instead / Ed, bed, fed, led, Ned, red, Ted, wed, bled, fled, sled, co-ed / said

12 **Dictation**

1. a package of (hotdogs) and a (bag) of chips
2. a dozen (eggs) and a (carton) of (milk)
3. (some) (fruit) and lots of (coffee)
4. a loaf of (bread) and a (few) bars of soap
5. jar of (jam), (package) of soup, 1 (box) of cereal
6. a bottle of (shampoo)

13 **Dictation**

1. something that goes (crunch)
2. a (box) of (crunchy) chips
3. a bunch of (grapes)
4. five (bunches) (of) green onions
5. a (box) of (pancake) mix
6. (canned) ham

unit 5 • **home** • Fix It Up

14 **Possible Responses:** beck, deck, heck, neck, peck, fleck, wreck / tech / cheque

15 **Possible Responses:** ace, face, lace, mace, pace, race, grace, trace / base, case, vase, chase

Possible Responses: bay, day, gay, hay, Jay, Kay, lay, may, say, way, bray, clay, play, pray, stay, tray / hey, grey / neigh, weigh, sleigh / eh

 Possible responses: by, my, dry, fly, fry, try, why / dye, rye / die, lie, pie, tie / high, sigh / buy, guy / bye / hi / eye / aye

 Possible responses: bank, Hank, sank, tank, blank, clank, crank, drank, Frank, plank, prank, spank, stank

17 Dictation

Hi Dad,

1. I'm finally in my new place, but I'm not very happy!
2. I have to (clean) and (fix) everything.
3. The sink has a (clog). I can't (remove) it.
4. The (paint) is (old) and dirty.
5. The rug is all (dusty). It has a big (rip).
6. I have to (replace) the windows because there is a big (draft).
7. The tub is (leaky). It has no (plug).
8. I still have to (check) a lot of things.
9. How can I (pay) for these things? (Please) help!

Your sad, sad son,
Jay

18 Dictation

1. fix the (rug)
2. fix (clogged) sink
3. fix (ripped) curtain
4. fix (plugged) drain
5. fix (drafty) door
6. fix (creaky) stairs
7. (strip) walls
8. (repaint) walls

23 Dictation

Hi Sis,

I need your help!

1. We want to (move) this (month).
2. I have (one) week to (rent) a place.
3. I (want) to (look) for a place with more (room).
4. I'm going to have to (carry) and (lug) tons of (boxes).
5. I want to (cry). Help!
6. Do you have time to fly down and help us (pack)?
7. I gave (notice) to the landlord last week.
8. They are still (fixing) the furnace.
9. There is no (gas) and no (heat)!
10. I have to get out of this (dive)!
11. Let me know if you can come. (Thank) you.

Deb

unit 6 • **home** • Changes

 Possible responses: back, hack, jack, lack, rack, sack, tack, wack, black, clack, crack, flack, knack, quack, slack, snack, stack, track / Mac / yak

 Possible responses: book, cook, hook, nook, rook, took, brook, crook, shook, mistook

Dictation

Hi Sis,

It's me again with good news!

1. We (moved) last week.
2. We (have) a (house)!
3. I (love) it!
4. I (walked*) to work today.
5. I (carry) my things in a (backpack).
6. There is a little (yard).
7. (You) have to see it.
8. I was (lugging) boxes for three days.
9. I feel like a (shaker) and (mover) now.
10. (Wishes) do come true!

Sorry to hear about your leg. Take care.

I miss you.

Deb

*walked: The **ed** ending has three pronunciations in English:
• **t** as in **walked**, **wished**, **noticed**
• **d** as in **moved**, **played**, **timed**
• **id** as in **rested**, **visited**, **needed**

Although the **ed** ending has different pronunciations, it is spelled the same because it is used to make (1) the past tense and (2) adjectives (e.g. **tired**, **pleased**, **bored**); therefore, its spelling is meaning-based, not sound-based. Base words that end in **t** or **d** have the distinct **id** sound.

unit 7 • community • Things to do

 Possible responses: Dick, hick, lick, Nick, pick, Rick, sick, tick, wick, click, flick, prick, quick, slick, stick, trick / Bic, tic

Possible responses: bow, low, mow, row, tow, blow, crow, flow, glow, grow, know, slow, snow, stow / foe, hoe, Joe, toe, woe / dough, though, although / go, no, so, pro / sew / oh

 Possible responses: down, gown, clown, crown, drown, frown / noun

Possible responses: dike, hike, like, Mike, pike, trike / tyke / psyche

 Dictation

There was always something to do when I was a kid.

1. In the (summer), we played (baseball) or (kick)-the-can.
2. We rode our (bikes) all the time.
3. We had (swimming) (classes).
4. We played all kinds of (sports).
5. The best of all was (fishing) in the pond.
6. In the (winter) we would (skate) on the pond.
7. Sometimes, we took the (bus) to (town).
8. We went (bowling) or to a (show). We looked in the (shop) windows.

Things have changed a lot!

Dictation

1. Kids don't play (pick)-up baseball.
2. (Biking) is not cool.
3. (They) spend a lot of time in (shopping) malls.
4. (Shows) cost a (lot) of money.
5. (Downtown) is not (safe) at night.
6. What (can) kids (do)?

unit 8 • community • Action

Possible responses: all, ball, call, fall, gall, mall, tall, wall, small, stall / loll, doll / haul, Paul / crawl, shawl

Possible responses: beet, feet, fleet, greet, sheet, sleet, street / eat, beat, heat, meat, neat, seat, cheat, treat, wheat / Pete

33 Possible responses: deed, feed, heed, seed, teed, weed, creed, greed, proceed, succeed / bead, lead, read, plead / precede

34 Dictation
1. We know you are (busy).
2. But, we (need) your (vote).
3. The (plan) is to (meet) for a (rally).
4. We will meet at (city) (hall).
5. The Pizza Place will (donate) (food).
6. Drinks will be on (sale).
7. You may win a (door) prize!
8. (Help) us (drive) out crime!
9. (Phone): 888-Fight

35 Dictation
Hi Jen,
1. Remember the rally I (talked) about?
2. I never (made) it. I (hit) a (bus).
3. I (planned) to get there on (time).
4. I (phoned) Sandy.
5. She (wanted) to (come).
6. I was (driving) along.
7. I was (making) good time.
8. (Then) - bam! (There) was (this) bus!
9. No more (rallies)* for me.
Jake

*Reminder: Add **es** so that pronunciation is maintained. Compare **rallis** and **rallies**.

unit 9 • community • Relations

36 Possible responses: dock, hock, jock, lock, mock, rock, sock, clock, crock, frock, knock, shock, stock / gawk, hawk / talk, walk, chalk, stalk / wok

37 Possible responses: bake, cake, fake, Jake, lake, make, rake, wake, awake, quake, stake / break, steak / ache

38 Possible responses: ice, dice, lice, mice, rice, vice, price, slice, splice, twice, advice, entice

39 Dictation
(Hi) Jane,
1. I go to a (club) now.
2. It's down the (block).
3. I (know) a lot of (people) there.
4. It's in the (church) basement.
5. I have a lot of (nice) (pals).
6. They (teach) me a lot.
7. It's like (school).
8. One (cop) is a (buddy) of mine.
9. It's good to (reach) out to people.
(Take) (care),
Dad

40 Dictation
Hi Dad,
1. I'm (glad) you have new (buddies).*
2. You seem (happier).
3. I'm (taking) care of my neighbour's (dog).
4. My neighbour (went) to (see) her boyfriend.
5. The dog's name is (Rocky).
6. He (knows) my neighbour (is) away.
7. He gets (sadder) every day.
8. We'll both be happy (when) she (comes) home.
9. See (you),
Jane

*Reminder: Add **es** so that pronunciation is maintained. Compare **buddis** and **buddies**.

unit 10 • community • Changes

 Possible responses: fight, might, night, right, sight, tight, blight, bright, flight, fright, knight, plight, slight / bite, kite, lite, quite, sprite, trite, white, write / height

 Possible responses: ear, dear, fear, gear, hear, near, rear, tear, year, smear, spear / beer, deer, jeer, leer, peer, seer, veer, cheer, queer, sneer, steer / pier, tier / here, mere / we're

 Dictation
Dear Mayor:
Our area looks bad!
We need to ...
1. • (Clear) out the (empty) (lots).
2. • (Shut) down the bars.
3. • (Put) up (new) (street) signs and (lights).
4. • (Plant) more trees and (shrubs).
5. • (Pave) the (roads).
6. • Make the roads (wider).
7. • (Build) a rec. centre.
8. Then let's watch our land (prices) go up!
Tim Dakin

 Dictation
Dear Tim Dakin:
1. We don't need more (buildings).
2. We don't need more (lighting).
3. We need to think in the (right) way.
4 (Paving) roads is (nice).
5. (Making) streets wider is (fine).
6. (But) we need (more) community (pride).
7. (That) starts (with) (putting) people first!
Lin Yung

unit 11 • work • Forms

 Possible responses: ill, bill, dill, fill, gill, hill, Jill, kill, mill, pill, sill, till, will, chill, drill, frill, grill, quill, shrill, spill, still, swill, thrill / Lil, nil, until

 Possible responses: by, my, cry, dry, fly, fry, why / dye, rye / die, lie, pie, tie / high, sigh / buy, guy / bye / hi / eye / aye

 Possible responses: bike, dike, hike, Mike, pike, trike / tyke / psyche

Dictation
1. Address: 25 Main (St.) / (Apt.) 14
2. Contact: 113 Haven (Rd.)
3. Birthdate: (April) 9, 1960
4. I have computer (skills).
5. I (work) well with people.
6. I (like) to (try) new (things)
7. I (learn) fast on the (job).
8. (Start): (Jan.) 2000
9. (Finish): (March) 2000

Dictation
1. I'm a fast (learner).
2. I have good (people) skills.
3. I have (started) (taking) computer (classes).
4. I (finished) (my) high school.
5. I'm a (good) (worker).
6. I'm (trying) to find a (night) job.
7. I know (Spanish).
8. I like (biking) and (working) (out).

unit 12 • work • Routines

 Possible responses: boon, goon, loon, moon, soon, croon, spoon / dune, June, tune

Possible responses: back, hack, jack, lack, pack, rack, sack, tack, wack, black, clack, crack, flack, knack, quack, slack, stack, track / Mac, yak

Possible Responses: bay, gay, hay, Jay, Kay, lay, may, say, way, bray, clay, pray, stay, tray / hey, grey / neigh, weigh, sleigh / eh

 Possible Responses: ace, lace, mace, pace, race, grace, place, trace / base, case, vase, chase

Dictation
1. I have the (day) (shift) at a donut shop.
2. We (never) have to (sign) in or out.
3. I have a (break) every hour.
4. I have (soup) at (noon) for (lunch).
5. I'll have a doughnut (snack) later.
6. I see the same (faces) every (morning).
7. We (always) (joke) and (laugh).
8. We (play) tricks on each other.
9. I like the routine.
10. It makes me feel safe.

Dictation
1. I (work) the (afternoon) shift.
2. We get a (five)-minute break every (two) hours.
3. (Sometimes), I sneak a (smoke).
4. (There) is no time for (playing) around.
5. The cars on the (line) keep going (by).
6. (They) never stop. No time (off).
7. It's like (one) long (replay).
8. (This) job is (killing) me.

unit 13 • work • Memo Board

 Possible responses: bell, fell, hell, Nell, tell, well, yell, shell, smell, spell, swell / gel, Mel

Possible responses: bound, hound, mound, pound, round, sound, around, ground / clowned (around), renowned

Possible responses: boy, coy, joy, Roy, soy, cloy, enjoy / buoy

Dictation
1. (Used) car for sale
2. (Lost) and (Found)
3. (Free) to a good home
4. (Best) (Offer)
5. Child's (toy) to (give) (away)
6. (Cheap) and in good (shape)
7. We (buy) and (sell)
8. (Wanted): Ride to work

Dictation
1. Wanted: (Buyers) and (Sellers)
2. (Cheaper) Better (Bigger)
3. Looking (for) give-(aways)
4. (Want) to trade (toys)?
5. (Giving) away (puppies)*.
6. Stereo for sale: Good (sound)
7. Call (from) 6 (to) 11 p.m.
8. (Tell) me (what) you need!

*Add **es** so that pronunciation is maintained. Compare **puppis** and **puppies**.

unit 14 • work • Relations

 Possible responses: jingle, single, tingle, shingle, Kringle

Possible responses: ear, dear, fear, gear, hear, near, rear, tear, clear, smear, spear / beer, deer, jeer, leer, peer, seer, veer, cheer, queer, sneer, steer / pier, tier / here, mere / we're

 Dictation
1. It's the (staff) (Christmas) party.
2. It's the biggest (event) of the (year)!
3. Meet the (bosses).
4. Play (games).
5. (Win) prizes!
6. (Where) is it? It's in Block 33.
7. When is it? (Saturday).
8. (Who) can say no to this?
9. (Enjoy)! (Stay) all day!
10. (Mix)! (Mingle)! (Relax)!

Dictation

1. Are you a good (runner)?
2. Do you like (playing) games?
3. Would you like a fun (relaxing)* day?
4. (Just) sign (your) (name).
5. Have no (fear)!
6. (So) (come) on and take (part).
7. When? (Saturdays) from 9 a.m. to noon.
8. Who (knows)?
9. You (might) (be) a big (winner)!

*Reminder: **xx** is not a possible combination in English.

unit 15 • **health** • General

 Possible responses: gain, main, rain, vain, drain, grain, plain, sprain, stain, strain, train / bane, cane, Dane, Jane, lane, mane, pane, sane, vane, crane, plane, inane, insane / deign, feign, reign / Wayne / Maine

 Possible responses: oat, boat, coat, goat, moat, bloat, float, gloat / dote, note, quote, rote, tote, vote, wrote

 Possible responses: hack, jack, lack, pack, rack, sack, tack, wack, black, clack, crack, flack, knack, quack, slack, snack, stack, track / Mac / yak

 Possible responses: Dick, hick, kick, lick, Nick, pick, Rick, tick, wick, click, flick, prick, quick, slick, stick, trick / Bic, tic

Dictation

1. I am (sick) and in (bed).
2. I have a (sore) (throat).
3. My (head) (hurts).
4. I feel (hot). I have a (fever).
5. I (ache) all over.
6. I have a (pain) in my (back).
7. I'm taking (drugs).
8. I (hope) to feel (better) soon.
9. I should go for a (test).

 Dictation

1. I (am) a lot better.
2. No more (aches) and (pains).
3. My (headache) is gone.
4. (My) back is not (aching).
5. I (stayed) in bed.
6. I (rested) (all) day.
7. That (was) the (trick)!

unit 16 • **health** • Diet

 Possible responses: ink, brink, fink, kink, link, mink, pink, rink, sink, wink, clink, slink, stink, think / zinc

 Possible responses: heat, neat, seat, treat, wheat / beet, feet, meet, fleet, greet, sheet, sleet, street / Pete

 Possible responses: book, hook, look, nook, rook, took, brook, crook, shook, mistook

Dictation

1. (Eat) (fresh) (greens).
2. Cut down on red (meat).
3. (Cook) more (fish) and (chicken).
4. (Drink) (water) and fruit (juice).
5. Say no to (sugar), (gravy), and (fats).
6. Don't buy (candy).
7. Watch your (diet). Live to be a hundred!

Dictation

1. My dad (eats) meat everyday.
2. He (loves) (fatty) food.
3. He (snacks) all the time.
4. He (thinks) (candies)* (are) great.
5. He never eats (fruit).
6. My dad is 99 (years) old.
7. (How) did he (get) to be so old?
8. (This) (dieting) stuff is (fishy).

*Reminder: Add **es** so that pronunciation is maintained.
Compare: **candis** and **candies**

unit 17 • health • Fitness

 76 **Possible responses:** gout, lout, pout, rout, about, shout, snout, spout, stout, trout / doubt

77 **Possible responses:** beep, deep, jeep, peep, seep, weep, bleep, cheep, creep, steep / heap, leap, reap

78 **Possible responses:** less, mess, bless, cress, dress, press, address, confess / Wes, yes

79 **Dictation**
1. How to stay (fit) and (trim).
2. Your (body) needs care.
3. (Sleep) when you are (tired).
4. Do all (kinds) of exercise.
5. Go for a (workout).
6. (Run), (jog), or (hike).
7. Cut down on (stress).
8. Don't (smoke).
9. (Keep) (mind) and (self) fit.

80 **Dictation**
1. (Keeping) fit.
2. What (does) this mean?
3. It means more than (jogging).
4. It means (more) than (running).
5. It means more (than) not (smoking).
6. Keeping fit means thinking (about) (your) needs.
7. It means being (nice) to (yourself).

unit 18 • health • Changes

 81 **Possible responses:** should, would / good, hood, wood, stood

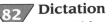 **82** **Dictation**
1. Did my (life) ever (change)!
2. My (partner) left me.
3. I did not (expect) it.
4. I (felt) (stunned).
5. I was (sad) and (lonely).
6. I was (tempted) to give up.
7. What (could) I do?
8. I had to (cope) and (recover).
9. I had to start (again).
10. I started to (rethink) my life.
11. I started to (discover) a new life.

 83 **Dictation**
1. I was (coping).
2. I started (walking) in the mornings.
3. (Other) people were walking, too.
4. (In) a few (months), we were friends.
5. They (were) my (friends) of the dawn.
6. There was (hope).
7. I (would) survive the break-up!

unit 19 • writings • Lists

 84 **Possible responses:** all, ball, fall, gall, hall, mall, tall, wall, small, stall / loll, doll / haul, Paul / crawl, shawl

 85 **Possible responses:** deed, heed, need, seed, teed, weed, creed, greed, proceed, succeed / bead, lead, read, plead / precede

86 **Possible responses:** Hank, sank, tank, blank, clank, crank, drank, Frank, plank, prank, spank, stank, thank

 87 **Possible responses:** ail, bail, fail, hail, jail, nail, pail, rail, sail, tail, flail, grail, quail, snail, trail / ale, Dale, pale, sale, tale, tale, stale, whale / Braille / veil

Dictation
1. (go) to (bank)
2. (feed) fish - (call) vet
3. (return) videos
4. (mail) (present) - buy (stamps)
5. (wash) out socks
6. (send) (fax) to Max
7. (remind) Hank to pick (up) (wedding) (gift)

 Dictation
1. (need) (more) stamps
2. stop (at) (mall) - (banking)
3. buy (nails) for pictures
4. send (thank) (you) card
5. (reminder): (shift) change today
6. (turn) (on) (washer) before (going) to work
7. (relax) after a hard day

unit 20 • writings • Dear Diary

 Possible responses: bow, cow, how, now, pow, sow, vow, meow / Tao

Possible responses: ear, fear, near, rear, tear, year, clear, spear / beer, deer, leer, peer, seer, veer, queer, sneer, steer / pier / here

Possible responses: caw, jaw, law, paw, raw, claw, craw, draw, flaw, gnaw, / ah, blah / ha, ma, pa / awe

Dictation
1. (Dear) Diary,
2. (Wow)!
3. (Today) was (very) strange.
4. I (went) to work.
5. (Everyone) (there) seemed weird.
6. They (seemed) to (ignore) me.
7. I (saw) Bonny.
8. I (said), "What's up?"
9. Bonny (says), "Oh, (nothing)."
10. I hope (tomorrow) isn't the (same).

Dictation
Dear Diary,
1. Things are not as bad (as) they (seem).
2. I (got) (to) work today.
3. Everyone starts (singing) "Happy Birthday."
4. (They) had a cake (and) (everything).
5. I (will) never forget (how) I felt.

unit 21 • writings • Notes

 Possible Responses: bay, day, gay, hay, Jay, Kay, lay, may, bray, clay, play, pray, stay, tray / hey, grey / neigh, weigh, sleigh / eh

 Possible responses: bell, fell, hell, Nell, sell, tell, yell, shell / gel, Mel

Dictation
1. (Howdy) there, Letty!
2. Just a (card) to (say) "(Well) (done)."
3. We (hear) you got a new job.
4. (Way) to go! (Good) work!
5. You (must) be so (excited).
6. We are so (proud) of you.
7. But, (sorry) to see you go.
8. (Let) us know how the job (goes).
Tony and the boys

Dictation
Hi Tony,
1. (How) do you like the (postcard)?
2. (The) job is pretty (hard).
3. Will (tell) you more (later).
4. (It) is (all) pretty (exciting).
5. I'm (near) the sea.
6. It's just a minute (away).
7. Say hi to (everyone) for (me).
Letty